THE ULTIMATE
CINCINNATI BENGALS
TRIVIA BOOK

A Collection of Amazing Trivia Quizzes
and Fun Facts for Die-Hard Bungles Fans!

Ray Walker

Exclusive Free Book
Crazy Sports Stories

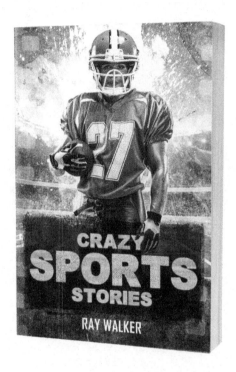

As a thank you for getting a copy of this book I would like to offer you a free copy of my book Crazy Sports Stories which comes packed with interesting stories from your favorite sports such as Football, Hockey, Baseball, Basketball and more.

Grab your free copy over at
RayWalkerMedia.com/Bonus

CONTENTS

INTRODUCTION

The history of the Cincinnati Bengals is checkered with some incredible moments and some tough lows. At its best, Cincinnati came within a few points of winning two—and maybe more—Super Bowls, but, at their worst, the Bengals lived up to their reputation as a tough franchise to play for. Even in recent years, the lack of success in the postseason has been a challenge for fans, who continue to get excited about their team's success. Despite some tension between players and management, some great players have come through Cincinnati, from Corey Dillon and Chad Johnson to Anthony Muñoz, Ken Anderson, and Boomer Esiason.

This trivia book features 12 chapters designed to test you as it spans the entire history of the Cincinnati Bengals from the good to the...well...not so good. Each chapter focuses on a different topic about the franchise, quizzing you on specific position groups as well as the team's history. Each chapter contains 20 multiple-choice or true-false questions, the answers to those questions on a separate page, followed by 10 interesting tidbits about that chapter's topic. Within these pages are plenty of fun facts and interesting nuggets that will challenge even the biggest Bengals fans, so please do not be alarmed if some of these questions stump you. The whole point of the book is to help you learn more about your favorite team, so we're successful if you finish this book knowing far more about the Bengals than when you began reading this page.

We hope you have learned something new after devouring this book, whether it's gradually over time or in just one sitting. Hopefully, you will use your newfound knowledge to show off to your fellow Bengals fans, whether you live in Ohio or anywhere else in the world. All of the information conveyed in this book is current as of the end of the 2020 season, so be warned that you might know more about the future by the time you pick up this book. All you need to do now is sit back, relax, and enjoy the hours of fun this book provides.

Who Dey!

CHAPTER 1:

ORIGINS & HISTORY

QUIZ TIME!

1. In what year did the American Football League award a franchise to Cincinnati?

    a. 1967
    b. 1968
    c. 1969
    d. 1970

2. Who was the original principal owner of the Bengals, who then sold his stake in the team to the Brown family in 1990?

    a. Jim Rhodes
    b. James Taft
    c. John Sawyer
    d. Woody Hayes

3. The fans in Cincinnati voted to name the team the "Buckeyes," but it was overruled by Paul Brown.

    a. True
    b. False

4. Which stadium hosted the Bengals for their first two seasons before Riverfront Stadium opened?

   a. League Park

   b. Crosley Field

   c. Nippert Stadium

   d. Cincinnati Gardens

5. When did the Bengals move into Paul Brown Stadium?

   a. 1990

   b. 1994

   c. 1997

   d. 2000

6. Which team faced Cincinnati in both the last regular-season game at Riverfront Stadium and the first regular-season game at Paul Brown Stadium?

   a. Tennessee Titans

   b. Pittsburgh Steelers

   c. Baltimore Ravens

   d. Cleveland Browns

7. Which team did Cincinnati face in its first regular-season game in the AFL?

   a. New York Jets

   b. San Diego Chargers

   c. Buffalo Bills

   d. Miami Dolphins

8. The Bengals did NOT win a road game during their first season in the AFL.

a. True

b. False

9. Which of the following teams did the Bengals NOT defeat during their inaugural season?

    a. Boston Patriots

    b. Buffalo Bills

    c. Miami Dolphins

    d. Denver Broncos

10. Who scored the first points in Bengals history?

    a. Jess Phillips

    b. Dale Livingston

    c. Tommie Smiley

    d. Paul Robinson

11. Who was the starting quarterback in Cincinnati's first regular-season game?

    a. Greg Cook

    b. Sam Wyche

    c. Dewey Warren

    d. John Stofa

12. Who has the most wins as the Bengals' starting quarterback?

    a. Jeff Blake

    b. Ken Anderson

    c. Boomer Esiason

    d. Andy Dalton

13. Which of these future NFL head coaches was never an assistant coach with the Bengals?

    a. Mike Zimmer
    b. Bill Walsh
    c. Sam Wyche
    d. Jay Gruden

14. More than half of the Bengals' head coaches after Paul Brown's tenure were previously assistant coaches in Cincinnati.

    a. True
    b. False

15. What was Paul Brown's final season as the Bengals' head coach?

    a. 1976
    b. 1975
    c. 1974
    d. 1973

16. Which of these Bengals' head coaches did NOT have a winning record while coaching in Cincinnati?

    a. Marvin Lewis
    b. Forrest Gregg
    c. Paul Brown
    d. Bill "Tiger" Johnson

17. What team did the Bengals face in their first playoff game after the 1970 season?

a. Los Angeles Raiders

b. Pittsburgh Steelers

c. Miami Dolphins

d. Baltimore Colts

18. Who scored the first postseason touchdown in Bengals history?

a. Boobie Clark

b. Charlie Joiner

c. Ken Anderson

d. Neal Craig

19. The Bengals have never made the playoffs without having at least a share of the division title.

a. True

b. False

20. What is the only team Cincinnati has defeated twice in the postseason?

a. Buffalo Bills

b. Los Angeles Chargers

c. Seattle Seahawks

d. Houston Texans

QUIZ ANSWERS

1. A – 1967

2. C – John Sawyer

3. A – True

4. C – Nippert Stadium

5. D – 2000

6. D – Cleveland Browns

7. B – San Diego Chargers

8. B – False

9. A – Boston Patriots

10. D – Paul Robinson

11. C – Dewey Warren

12. B – Ken Anderson

13. C – Sam Wyche

14. A – True

15. B – 1975

16. C – Paul Brown

17. D – Baltimore Colts

18. D – Neal Craig

19. B – False

20. A – Buffalo Bills

DID YOU KNOW?

1. Three years before the Bengals debuted in the AFL in 1968, discussions about their existence began between Paul Brown and Ohio governor Jim Rhodes. After the two agreed that the state could support a second professional football team, the Cincinnati City Council approved the construction of Riverfront Stadium in 1966, and Brown headed the group that would be awarded the franchise in Cincinnati to begin play in 1968.

2. Paul Brown settled on the "Bengals" nickname as an homage to the previous professional football team in the city. The original Bengals played from 1937 to 1941 in several different leagues, almost all of which were also called the American Football League. The previous franchise had a mixed bag of success before folding in 1941 along with the league, with the threat of World War II looming over the country. However, before deciding on the "Bengals," the team held an informal poll, and "Buckeyes" was the overwhelming favorite for the team's nickname. Brown said that the name belonged to Ohio State and that "Buckeyes" wasn't going to be popular with the regional fan base he hoped to grow in Indiana, Kentucky, and West Virginia.

3. The Bengals are one of the few franchises that are still owned by the same family that founded the team. Paul

Brown was the controlling owner for the Bengals from their inception in 1968 until his death in 1991, when his son, Mike Brown, took over. Ever since Paul Brown was awarded the team, he or his son has served as the general manager of the franchise, controlling every aspect of football operations for the organization. The only non-Brown to have any say in the executive branch was John Sawyer, who served as team president from 1968 to 1993 as Brown's right-hand man. Sawyer helped build Riverfront Stadium and also was a minority owner in the Bengals.

4. The 1968 Bengals had Hall-of-Famer Bill Walsh on their staff. He coached the receivers and ends for three seasons before moving to coach the quarterbacks from 1971 to 1975. Walsh is one of three assistants on that inaugural staff who went on to be a head coach in the NFL, joining Bill Johnson and Rick Forzano. Johnson is one of five Bengals assistants who were later promoted to head coach, therefore accounting for half of the head coaches in franchise history. In addition to Johnson, Bruce Coslet, Dick LeBeau, Homer Rice, and Dave Shula were assistants before being promoted.

5. Cincinnati had an excellent start to its first regular-season game as a professional football franchise, marching down the field on the opening possession to score on a Paul Robinson two-yard touchdown run. Unfortunately, that was about as well as it would go for the Bengals in San Diego that day, as the Chargers rallied for a 29-13 win.

The following week, however, the Bengals opened up their home slate with a 24-10 win over the Broncos at Nippert Stadium for one of their three wins during their inaugural season.

6. The Bengals made history in 1970, their first year in the NFL, by winning the AFC Central Division with an 8-6 record. They became the first expansion franchise to win a championship of any kind in just three years or fewer. Their playoff debut did not last long, though, as they were shut out 17-0 by the Colts in the divisional round, and Cincinnati had to wait a dozen years until they won their first postseason contest as a franchise.

7. Sam Wyche was a colorful character who made headlines for the right and wrong reasons while coaching the Bengals. He has the second-most wins of any Bengals coach, and he led the team to one of its two appearances in the Super Bowl with his innovative no-huddle offense headed by quarterback Boomer Esiason. However, he was also in the middle of controversy at times, including when he barred females from the Bengals' locker room and when he insulted the entire city of Cleveland when Cincinnati fans pelted the officials with snowballs during a 1989 game. His last four words of his immortal speech that closed, "You don't live in Cleveland. You live in Cincinnati," are permanently etched on the side of Paul Brown Stadium as a reminder of the team's connection to the city.

8. Marvin Lewis could be seen as a controversial figure in Cincinnati sports history for his longevity despite subpar results. Lewis had a magnificent run with the Bengals statistically, leading the franchise to seven of the team's 14 playoff berths in their history, including four division crowns in the tough AFC North. He is the franchise's winningest coach with 131 victories in 16 years as the team's coach, after walking into a tough situation with a playoff drought that he ended at 14 years in his third season at the helm. But many fans were critical of the team's lack of success in the playoffs as Lewis lost all seven postseason games he coached with the Bengals, who were outscored 176-90 in those games.

9. The Bengals have a slight edge in the Battle for Ohio with a 51-44 record against the Cleveland Browns. However, Cincinnati has not had much luck against the rest of the division or the AFC. It has losing records to 12 of the other 13 AFC teams, with the exception being its 15-14 record in 29 matchups with Kansas City. Within their own division, the Bengals are 23-27 against the Ravens and 36-65 against the Steelers. The only other team Cincinnati has played at least 50 times is the Tennessee Titans, and the Bengals are 34-40-1 against that franchise, dating back to the Titans' history as the Houston Oilers.

10. Though the city began building Riverfront Stadium as a home for the Cincinnati Reds of Major League Baseball and the then-unnamed AFL franchise in 1967, construction wasn't going to be completed until 1970.

Therefore, the Bengals played their first two seasons on the campus of the University of Cincinnati at Nippert Stadium. The Bengals played at Riverfront Stadium for 30 seasons, from 1970 to 1999, until moving a quarter mile west to the site of Paul Brown Stadium, which has hosted the Bengals since 2000.

CHAPTER 2:

NUMBERS GAME

QUIZ TIME!

1. Who is the only player whose number has been retired by the Bengals franchise?

    a. Bob Johnson

    b. Ken Anderson

    c. Anthony Muñoz

    d. Boomer Esiason

2. What is the only number that has never been worn by any Bengals in a regular-season game?

    a. 16

    b. 8

    c. 2

    d. 1

3. Who was the first player in Bengals history to wear a single-digit number?

    a. Jeff Hayes

    b. Monk Williams

c. James Pearson

d. Boomer Esiason

4. Who wore number 7 for the Bengals between Boomer Esiason's two tenures with the franchise?

   a. Doug Pelfrey

   b. Jeff Blake

   c. David Klingler

   d. Erik Wilhelm

5. Which number did Ken Riley wear while playing defensive back for the Bengals?

   a. 34

   b. 23

   c. 13

   d. 6

6. No one wore number 14 between Ken Anderson's retirement and Andy Dalton's arrival in Cincinnati.

   a. True

   b. False

7. Which number was worn by both Paul Robinson and Charlie Joiner during their careers in Cincinnati?

   a. 28

   b. 21

   c. 18

   d. 10

8. Who has NOT worn number 28 since the Bengals traded Corey Dillon?

a. Bernard Scott

b. Dexter Jackson

c. Joe Mixon

d. Giovanni Bernard

9. What number did Ickey Woods wear for the first eight games of the 1988 season before switching to number 30?

a. 20

b. 31

c. 34

d. 40

10. What number did Archie Griffin wear for the Bengals?

a. 38

b. 41

c. 43

d. 45

11. Which number was worn by the only Hall-of-Famer to play most of his career with the Bengals?

a. 70

b. 73

c. 76

d. 78

12. Isaac Curtis and Chad Johnson wore the same number with the Bengals.

a. True

b. False

13. Which current Bengals player shares the same number as Reggie Williams?

    a. Billy Price
    b. Josh Bynes
    c. Germaine Pratt
    d. Carl Lawson

14. Which number did Coy Bacon and Ross Browner wear during their time in Cincinnati?

    a. 95
    b. 75
    c. 94
    d. 79

15. What number did Dan Ross wear when he returned to the Bengals from the World Football League in 1985?

    a. 84
    b. 86
    c. 87
    d. 89

16. What number does Geno Atkins wear for the Bengals?

    a. 91
    b. 94
    c. 97
    d. 99

17. The Bengals wore white helmets in their inaugural season before changing them to orange in the second year.

a. True

b. False

18. In which year did the Bengals add tiger stripes to their helmets?

    a. 1981

    b. 1977

    c. 1972

    d. 1968

19. The first time the Bengals wore orange uniforms was in the twenty-first century.

    a. True

    b. False

20. What is written on the inside of the uniform collar in the Bengals' 2021 uniform redesign?

    a. "Cincinnati"

    b. Paul Brown's signature

    c. "Be the Roar"

    d. "Who Dey"

QUIZ ANSWERS

1. A – Bob Johnson

2. D – 1

3. B – Monk Williams

4. C – David Klingler

5. C – 13

6. B – False

7. C – 18

8. D – Giovanni Bernard

9. B – 31

10. D – 45

11. D – 78

12. A – True

13. C – Germaine Pratt

14. D – 79

15. A – 84

16. C – 97

17. B – False

18. A – 1981

19. A – True

20. B – Paul Brown's signature

DID YOU KNOW?

1. Bob Johnson is the only player to have his number officially retired by the Bengals. The team honored the longtime center after his final game in 1978 by retiring his jersey, making Johnson the only Bengals player to ever wear the number 54. Though Johnson's number is the only one officially retired, no Bengals player has worn Anthony Muñoz's number 78 since the offensive lineman retired in 1992.

2. Boomer Esiason grew up a Colts fan and owned a Johnny Unitas jersey for much of his childhood. But he chose to wear number 7 on the football field because of his love and admiration for Bert Jones, who replaced Unitas as the Colts' starting quarterback in 1973.

3. Ken Anderson wore number 14 for 16 seasons in Cincinnati, and the number was held in reserve after Anderson retired in 1986. Receiver Maurice Purify wore the jersey for five games in 2009, but most Bengals fans likely remember Andy Dalton accepting the onus of the number after he was drafted in 2011. When Anderson phoned Dalton to give him his approval to wear number 14, Anderson told Dalton that he better be good, an expectation Dalton lived up to during his tenure with the Bengals.

4. Cris Collinsworth was battling some injuries during the 1987 season, so he was quite literally replaced in the uniform number 80 for two games. Collinsworth wore number 80 for his entire eight-season career in Cincinnati, but, for two games in 1987, Tom Brown was listed as number 80 while Collinsworth was dealing with injuries. Collinsworth wore the number for the first two games of the season and then again from the sixth through the 15th contest, but Brown was number 80 for the fourth and fifth games of the season.

5. For a brief period, Chad Johnson's jersey number became his actual legal name. It all began in 2006 when Johnson put the name "Ocho Cinco" on his jersey to signify his number 85 during pregame warm-ups for a game during Hispanic Heritage Month. The name was ripped off before kickoff, but Johnson was still fined. In 2008, he legally changed his name to Chad Ocho Cinco in honor of his uniform number, a stunt he undid in 2012.

6. It would make sense that Hardy Nickerson Jr. purposefully chose number 56 when he joined the Bengals in 2017 to honor his father. However, it was a complete coincidence that the Cincinnati linebacker is wearing the same number his father did when he was playing in the NFL. Nickerson had just chosen the number because he thought it was a good number for a linebacker, forgetting about the tradition his father brought to the number as a four-time All-Pro and five-time Pro Bowler.

7. For whatever reason, the single-digit numbers have never been very popular in Bengals history. Monk Williams wore number 6 on the inaugural 1968 team, but no other single-digit number was worn until 1984 when Boomer Esiason wore number 7. In fact, no Bengals player has ever worn number 1, though that may change in 2021 as the NFL passed new uniform rules that open the number to more position groups. Only two players have ever worn number 2, and Joe Burrow was the fifth player in franchise history to wear number 9.

8. In July 2020, CBS Sports unveiled its list of the best players in NFL history to wear every uniform number. The only Bengals player to make the list was Anthony Muñoz, representing number 78, though Boomer Esiason was considered for number 7, and Ken Anderson was an honorable mention for number 14.

9. The tiger stripes were added to the Bengals' helmets in 1981, distinguishing Cincinnati's helmets far more than the previous versions. Paul Brown said of the change, "You couldn't read 'Bengals' on our helmet from a distance. When you were far away, it looked like Cleveland's helmet." For the first 13 seasons of play, the Bengals simply had "Bengals" written in block letters on an orange helmet, which may have been different than the Browns' helmets but still looked similar enough. In 1981, Cincinnati went radical and added six tiger stripes to the orange helmet, and that tiger striping continued onto the jerseys and pants.

10. The Bengals added an orange jersey for the first time in 2004 as part of the second redesign of the uniforms. That year, Cincinnati also introduced black pants as an official part of the uniform, though the Bengals wore black pants in the season opener and season finale in 2003 as part of the redesign process. That design lasted 17 seasons before the Bengals rolled out a sleeker design for the 2021 season that simplified and enhanced the tiger stripes on the jersey and pants. The team also added Paul Brown's signature on the inside collar of each jersey to connect the team with its past.

CHAPTER 3:

CALLING THE SIGNALS

QUIZ TIME!

1. Who did NOT start at least one game for the Bengals in their inaugural season in 1968?

    a. Sam Wyche

    b. Greg Cook

    c. John Stofa

    d. Dewey Warren

2. Which Bengals quarterback was named both the Associated Press NFL MVP and the AP's Offensive Player of the Year in the same season?

    a. Carson Palmer

    b. Akili Smith

    c. Boomer Esiason

    d. Ken Anderson

3. Who made the most Pro Bowl appearances as a Bengals quarterback?

    a. Ken Anderson

    b. Boomer Esiason

c. Carson Palmer

d. Andy Dalton

4. There have been only four 4,000-yard passing seasons in Bengals history.

   a. True

   b. False

5. Who threw the most touchdown passes in a season in Bengals history?

   a. Ken Anderson

   b. Andy Dalton

   c. Carson Palmer

   d. Boomer Esiason

6. Which of these quarterbacks has at least 10 wins and a winning record as the Bengals' starting quarterback?

   a. Virgil Carter

   b. Jon Kitna

   c. Jeff Blake

   d. Turk Schonert

7. What is Ken Anderson's record for most completions in a single game?

   a. 33

   b. 37

   c. 40

   d. 42

8. Who threw the longest pass in Bengals history, a 94-yard touchdown?

a. Jon Kitna

b. Ken Anderson

c. Virgil Carter

d. Carson Palmer

9. No Bengals quarterback has rushed for more than 1,500 yards in his career.

a. True

b. False

10. Who does NOT share the Bengals' record of 22 interceptions in a season?

a. Jon Kitna

b. Ken Anderson

c. Boomer Esiason

d. Carson Palmer

11. In which two consecutive years did Ken Anderson lead the NFL in passing yards?

a. 1981 and 1982

b. 1978 and 1979

c. 1976 and 1977

d. 1974 and 1975

12. Ken Anderson set the Bengals' single-season record for completion percentage at 70.6% in 1982.

a. True

b. False

13. How many touchdown passes did Boomer Esiason throw in 1997 when he led the Bengals to four wins in their final five games before retiring?

    a. 10
    b. 11
    c. 12
    d. 13

14. What is Boomer Esiason's legal first name?

    a. Julius
    b. Gregory
    c. Norman
    d. William

15. In which season did Jon Kitna become the only Bengals player to be named the Associated Press Comeback Player of the Year?

    a. 2003
    b. 2002
    c. 2001
    d. 2000

16. In 2005, Carson Palmer led the NFL in passing touchdowns by tossing how many?

    a. 29
    b. 31
    c. 32
    d. 34

17. Carson Palmer did not throw a touchdown pass in his first win as a starting quarterback.

    a. True
    b. False

18. Which of these Bengals career records does Andy Dalton hold?

    a. Interceptions
    b. Completion percentage
    c. Completions
    d. Passing attempts

19. When did Andy Dalton set the Bengals' single-season record for passing yards in a season?

    a. 2016
    b. 2012
    c. 2015
    d. 2013

20. How many times did Joe Burrow throw for 300 yards in 10 starts in 2020 to tie the franchise record for most 300-yard performances in a season?

    a. 7
    b. 4
    c. 5
    d. 6

QUIZ ANSWERS

1. B – Greg Cook

2. D – Ken Anderson

3. A – Ken Anderson

4. A – True

5. B – Andy Dalton

6. A – Virgil Carter

7. C – 40

8. B – Ken Anderson

9. B – False

10. D – Carson Palmer

11. D – 1974 and 1975

12. A – True

13. D – 13

14. C – Norman

15. A – 2003

16. C – 32

17. B – False

18. C – Completions

19. D – 2013

20. C – 5

DID YOU KNOW?

1. When it comes to the quarterback position, the Bengals have had a relatively easy time finding their guy. They are the only franchise in the post-merger era to have four different quarterbacks start at least 97 games for the team that drafted them. That list is headed by Ken Anderson (192 starts) and includes Boomer Esiason (123 starts), Andy Dalton (133), and Carson Palmer (97). The hope is Joe Burrow will continue that legacy of longevity when he returns from his knee injury.

2. John Stofa played on two expansion teams during his career, starting as part of the original 1966 Miami Dolphins before joining the 1968 Bengals. He said the Bengals were in a far better position as an expansion franchise due to the leadership of Paul Brown, whose experience in the NFL helped avoid the chaos of a first season. Stofa was the first Bengals player in history and proudly held the honor by buying custom license plates when he moved to Ohio that read "1ST BNGL."

3. Ken Anderson is the only Bengals quarterback to lead the league in passing yards, doing so in 1974 and 1975, but he didn't lead the NFL—or even the AFC—in passing yards in 1981 when he was named the league MVP. In addition to winning every major MVP award in 1981, Anderson was also the Pro Football Writers Association's Comeback

Player of the Year after finishing fifth in the league in passing yards and third in passing touchdowns.

4. Despite retiring in 1987 from playing for the Bengals, Ken Anderson didn't stray too far from the only franchise for which he ever played. The month after he announced his retirement, Anderson signed on to be the color analyst on the Bengals' radio broadcast, a role he held for seven years before returning to the field as an assistant coach with the franchise. He spent 10 years on the Bengals' staff as the quarterbacks coach and/or offensive coordinator before coaching another seven seasons with other NFL teams.

5. Boomer Esiason was the man tasked with running Sam Wyche's no-huddle offense, which meant a lot of work for Esiason. Wyche was constantly quizzing and testing Esiason on the formations, play calls, and other details needed to run a no-huddle offense. And, unlike the no-huddle offenses in modern times, Wyche didn't allow Esiason to wear a wristband as a failsafe, demanding his quarterback know every inch of the playbook to quickly and efficiently call and execute the play.

6. Boomer Esiason's nickname actually predated his birth. The man born Norman Julius Esiason Jr. seemed to be more destined to be a kicker or soccer player than a quarterback in the womb with how much he kicked his mother. The excessive kicking earned him the nickname "Boomer" before he was born, and it stuck with him for his entire life.

7. Carson Palmer had plenty of success in Cincinnati, but his departure from the team in the middle of the 2011 season left a sour taste to those memories. Depending on the story you want to believe, Palmer was either dissatisfied enough with the Bengals' ownership that he demanded a trade and retired after the 2010 season, or he was concerned about his long-term future after that dismal 4-12 campaign. Either way, Palmer refused to report to training camp in 2011 and retired, but came out of retirement after being dealt in the middle of the 2011 campaign.

8. Andy Dalton's ginger hair made it easy for fans and teammates to come up with some type of nickname using the color red. The nickname most people settled on was the "Red Rifle," combining his hair color and position, but Dalton himself wasn't a big fan of the nickname. In 2011, he lamented, "It's all right. It seems like everybody is going to find a nickname with 'red' or something for my hair. So, the Red Rifle is alright." He said he prefers to just go by Andy.

9. For the Bengals, it was just a 49-yard touchdown pass that helped them beat the Ravens to cap off a disappointing 2017 season. But for the fans of the Buffalo Bills, Andy Dalton's toss was the end of a playoff drought, and the city of Cincinnati benefitted greatly from that pass. After the game, Bills fans flooded Andy Dalton's foundation, which provides resources for seriously ill and physically challenged children and their families in Cincinnati. The one pass led to more than $800,000 in donations to the

foundation, changing the lives of so many families in the Cincinnati area.

10. Joe Burrow took his lumps as a rookie quarterback behind a patchwork offensive line, but at least he kept a good sense of humor about it. In a Week 3 game against the Philadelphia Eagles, Burrow was rocked by a hit by Malik Jackson. Everyone was curious if the referees were going to flag Jackson for roughing the passer, including Burrow, who peeked at the field when he got up. When he saw there wasn't a flag on the play, Burrow told the Eagles' defense, "You know when I'm the GOAT, I'm going to get that call," causing a laugh from the defenders out of respect.

CHAPTER 4:

BETWEEN THE TACKLES

QUIZ TIME!

1. Who holds the Bengals' record for most rushing yards in a single season?

   a. Joe Mixon

   b. Corey Dillon

   c. Rudi Johnson

   d. Paul Robinson

2. Rudi Johnson never had a 200-yard rushing game for the Bengals.

   a. True

   b. False

3. How long was the longest rush in Cincinnati history?

   a. 96 yards

   b. 93 yards

   c. 89 yards

   d. 87 yards

4. Which of these running backs did NOT rush for at least 5,000 yards with the Bengals?

   a. Pete Johnson
   b. James Brooks
   c. Corey Dillon
   d. Cedric Benson

5. Who was the first Bengals running back to rush for 1,000 yards in a season?

   a. James Brooks
   b. Pete Johnson
   c. Paul Robinson
   d. Essex Johnson

6. Who is the only Bengals running back to rush for 100 yards in four consecutive games?

   a. Jeremy Hill
   b. Paul Robinson
   c. Corey Dillon
   d. James Brooks

7. Rudi Johnson is the last Bengal to be named a Pro Bowler at running back.

   a. True
   b. False

8. Who is the only Bengals running back to be named a First Team All-Pro?

   a. Ickey Woods
   b. Corey Dillon

c. Rudi Johnson

d. Paul Robinson

9. Whose 361 rushing attempts is a single-season record for Cincinnati?

    a. Corey Dillon

    b. BenJarvus Green-Ellis

    c. Rudi Johnson

    d. Cedric Benson

10. Which running back averaged 4.8 yards per carry during his career with the Bengals to set the franchise record?

    a. James Brooks

    b. Essex Johnson

    c. Joe Mixon

    d. Rudi Johnson

11. Paul Robinson had a scholarship in which sport for most of his career at the University of Arizona?

    a. Soccer

    b. Baseball

    c. Basketball

    d. Track and field

12. What is Pete Johnson's actual birth name?

    a. Petr Kozlov

    b. Peter Allen Johnson

    c. William Peter Jamieson

    d. Willie James Hammock

13. In which year did Pete Johnson have his only 1,000-yard season?

    a. 1979
    b. 1980
    c. 1981
    d. 1982

14. James Brooks is illiterate.

    a. True
    b. False

15. What is Ickey Woods's legal first name?

    a. Albert
    b. Elbert
    c. Ellington
    d. Isaac

16. How many times did Corey Dillon rush for 1,000 yards in a season for the Bengals?

    a. 6
    b. 5
    c. 4
    d. 3

17. How many times did Corey Dillon rush for 100 yards in a game during his career in Cincinnati?

    a. 22
    b. 26
    c. 28
    d. 31

18. Rudi Johnson never rushed for 10 touchdowns in a season for the Bengals.

   a. True
   b. False

19. In which season did the Bengals set their franchise record for most rushing yards as a team?

   a. 1982
   b. 1988
   c. 1994
   d. 2000

20. Who holds the Bengals' record for most rushing yards in a postseason game?

   a. Pete Johnson
   b. Rudi Johnson
   c. Ickey Woods
   d. Cedric Benson

QUIZ ANSWERS

1. C – Rudi Johnson

2. B – False

3. A – 96 yards

4. D – Cedric Benson

5. C – Paul Robinson

6. B – Paul Robinson

7. A – True

8. D – Paul Robinson

9. C – Rudi Johnson

10. A – James Brooks

11. D – Track and field

12. D – Willie James Hammock

13. C – 1981

14. A – True

15. B – Elbert

16. A – 6

17. C – 28

18. B – False

19. B – 1988

20. D – Cedric Benson

DID YOU KNOW?

1. Paul Robinson planned to go to the Air Force Academy, become the first in his family to earn a college degree, spend two decades serving his country, and then retire for a job in the private sector, which would earn him two pensions. That was always the plan, at least, until he arrived at Eastern Arizona Junior College. There, Robinson was the only athlete to qualify for the national championships in the intermediate hurdles, and he earned a track and field scholarship to the University of Arizona. He needed another year to get his degree, however, so he tried out for the football team to get a scholarship for his final year of school. He didn't want to play as much as earn that degree, but he did receive 80 carries and gained 306 yards due to injuries, and his natural athleticism caught the eye of Paul Brown, who then drafted Robinson and changed the trajectory of his life plan.

2. Pete Johnson is neither a Peter nor a Johnson by birth. When he was born in Georgia, his name was Willie James Hammock, and the story behind the name he had professionally depends on who you ask. The last name either came from his dad, his grandfather, President Lyndon B. Johnson, or Johnson & Johnson, the company that makes Band-Aids. As for Pete, his mother insists that was a nickname she had called him since he was two days

old, though the running back himself credits the name to his uncle calling him Pete due to his love for the Peter Pan ice cream trucks.

3. Though it never had an impact on his football abilities, James Brooks was legally illiterate, as the world found out after his playing career. It was a well-known secret throughout his football career in high school, in college at Auburn, and then with the Bengals that Brooks struggled to read, but he found other ways to produce on the field. He was extremely athletic, which helped, but teammates also said he used a different version of the playbook to learn his responsibilities for every play. That's all that mattered to his coaches and teammates as he played in four Pro Bowls during his time in Cincinnati.

4. Only three times in the Bengals' history has a non-kicker led the team in scoring, and in all three seasons, it was a running back who led the way. Pete Johnson was the first to accomplish the feat in 1979 when his 15 touchdowns and 90 points were the most on the team. Ickey Woods copied that feat in 1988 with the same 90 points on 15 touchdowns, and Corey Dillon scored 78 points on 13 touchdowns to lead the Bengals in scoring in 2001.

5. The Bengals drafted Ki-Jana Carter with the 1st overall pick in 1995, and it didn't take long for a curse to befall the running back. On his third carry for the Bengals, which came in the preseason opener in Detroit, Carter's left foot got caught in the carpet of the Silverdome and his knee

twisted, causing a torn ACL. He missed the entire 1995 season with that injury and then the injuries piled up, with a torn rotator cuff, a broken wrist, and a dislocated kneecap ending his next four seasons prematurely.

6. Corey Dillon's exit from Cincinnati was a difficult one, as bitter emotions tainted his final few seasons with the Bengals. The franchise's all-time leading rusher was frustrated with the team's direction from 2000 to 2003, and he aired those grievances very publicly. At one point, he even said he'd rather "flip burgers" than return for another season with the Bengals, and his final moment as a Bengals player was him chucking his shoulder pads into the seats at Paul Brown Stadium. However, the two sides have begun to mend the relationship. Dillon admitted in 2017 that "I am a grown man, I can admit when I'm wrong. I did some stuff that was not cool, okay? Not cool at all."

7. Rudi Johnson was a more than adequate replacement for Corey Dillon, rushing for 1,000 yards in three straight seasons from 2004 to 2006 until injuries took their toll. When renegotiating his contract in 2005, Johnson proved his commitment to the Bengals by taking less money than some other backs in the league to stay in Cincinnati. However, he never was able to live out the term of that 2005 contract as the Bengals released him in 2008 while Johnson was dealing with hamstring issues that forced him to miss most of training camp.

8. Cedric Benson's career blossomed for a brief bit in Cincinnati with three consecutive 1,000-yard seasons, from 2009 to 2011. However, Benson proved to not be a fit with the Bengals' culture, and the team declined to re-sign him in 2012 despite his recent success. When asked about the decision, then-Bengals coach Marvin Lewis said he told Benson, "Ced, it's not that I didn't think you could do that on the football field, it was the other [stuff] that I got tired of. When I would go to you and say we're going to rotate the backs [and Benson would take it poorly], I don't need that anymore."

9. Jeremy Hill burst onto the scene with the Bengals as a rookie in 2014, rushing for 1,124 yards in just eight starts for Cincinnati. He scored a career-best 11 touchdowns, tied for the most in the league the following season. He ran for nine more touchdowns in his third season in the league but failed to reach 1,000 yards in either his second or third year in the league before falling out of favor in 2017, and he eventually finished the year on injured reserve with an ankle injury.

10. When the Bengals drafted Joe Mixon in 2017, what came with the selection was the baggage of an assault charge from his freshman year at the University of Oklahoma. Cincinnati had done its due diligence on the issue, and Bengals owner Mike Brown even penned a letter to the community about the draft pick that was published in the local newspaper. The pick itself has been a successful one as Mixon ran for 1,000 yards in 2018 and 2019 and was on

pace for another 1,000-yard season in 2020 if not for injuries.

CHAPTER 5:

CATCHING THE BALL

QUIZ TIME!

1. Who is the only Bengals receiver to surpass 10,000 receiving yards during his career with Cincinnati?

   a. Isaac Curtis

   b. Chad Johnson

   c. A.J. Green

   d. T.J. Houshmandzadeh

2. Which of these receivers never had 200 receiving yards in a game for the Bengals?

   a. Cris Collinsworth

   b. Eddie Brown

   c. Terrell Owens

   d. T.J. Houshmandzadeh

3. No Bengals receiver has had more than six 100-yard games in a season.

   a. True

   b. False

4. Who has the most 100-yard performances in Bengals history, with 33?

   a. Chad Johnson
   b. T.J. Houshmandzadeh
   c. A.J. Green
   d. Carl Pickens

5. Who holds the Bengals' record for most receptions in a season, with 112?

   a. Chad Johnson
   b. Carl Pickens
   c. T.J. Houshmandzadeh
   d. A.J. Green

6. Which Bengals receiver never led the AFC in receiving yards during his career in Cincinnati?

   a. A.J. Green
   b. Eddie Brown
   c. Chad Johnson
   d. Isaac Curtis

7. Which of these Bengals receivers was NOT named to at least four Pro Bowls while playing in Cincinnati?

   a. Bob Trumpy
   b. Isaac Curtis
   c. Cris Collinsworth
   d. Chad Johnson

8. No Bengals wide receiver has ever been named a First Team All-Pro in multiple seasons.

a. True

b. False

9. Who is the Bengals' leader for career receiving yards by a tight end?

   a. Tyler Eifert

   b. Dan Ross

   c. Jermaine Gresham

   d. Bob Trumpy

10. Who was the last tight end to lead the Bengals in receiving?

   a. Dan Ross

   b. Rodney Holman

   c. Tyler Eifert

   d. Bob Trumpy

11. How many touchdown passes did Bob Trumpy catch in his career, the most by a tight end in Bengals history?

   a. 29

   b. 31

   c. 33

   d. 35

12. Isaac Curtis never played receiver during his college football career and entered the draft as a running back before converting to wide receiver.

   a. True

   b. False

13. Who was the first Bengals receiver to have 1,000 receiving yards in a season?

   a. Dan Ross
   b. Isaac Curtis
   c. Cris Collinsworth
   d. Billy Brooks

14. Who was the first Bengals player to be named the Offensive Rookie of the Year by the Associated Press?

   a. Eddie Brown
   b. Isaac Curtis
   c. Carl Pickens
   d. Cris Collinsworth

15. Which of these Bengals receivers led the team in receiving yards three times during his Cincinnati career?

   a. Peter Warrick
   b. T.J. Houshmandzadeh
   c. Bob Trumpy
   d. Darnay Scott

16. What is T.J. Houshmandzadeh's legal first name?

   a. Tirdad
   b. Terrance
   c. Touraj
   d. Tehran

17. Chad Johnson led the NFL in receiving yards the year before he set the current Bengals franchise record for receiving yards.

a. True

b. False

18. How many passes did Chad Johnson catch during his Bengals career to set the franchise record for receptions?

    a. 720

    b. 736

    c. 742

    d. 751

19. How many consecutive years did A.J. Green make the Pro Bowl to start his NFL career?

    a. 6

    b. 7

    c. 8

    d. 9

20. A.J. Green earned which nickname from his teammates for his otherworldly plays during practice and games?

    a. "The Astronaut"

    b. "The Martian"

    c. "ALF"

    d. "Captain Jupiter"

QUIZ ANSWERS

1. B – Chad Johnson

2. D – T.J. Houshmandzadeh

3. A – True

4. C – A.J. Green

5. C – T.J. Houshmandzadeh

6. A – A.J. Green

7. C – Cris Collinsworth

8. B – False

9. D – Bob Trumpy

10. A – Dan Ross

11. D – 35

12. B – False

13. C – Cris Collinsworth

14. A – Eddie Brown

15. D – Darnay Scott

16. C – Touraj

17. A – True

18. D – 751

19. B – 7

20. B – "The Martian"

DID YOU KNOW?

1. Bob Trumpy knew that his skinny figure would be an issue for the Bengals, who wanted him to play tight end, so he snuck a 10-pound weight into his pocket for weigh-ins, turning his 208-pound frame into a 218-pound frame. Trumpy needed all the help he could get as a 12th round draft pick for that inaugural team. He had six roommates during the first training camp, and all six were eventually cut before Trumpy was placed with center Bob Johnson, the only player from that first Bengals team in 1968 to play longer than Trumpy's 10 years with the franchise.

2. Isaac Curtis did a lot of things during his first three years in college, but playing receiver was not one of them. The legendary pass-catcher played three seasons at California as a running back and helped the Golden Bears win the national championship in track and field as a freshman. However, it wasn't until he transferred to San Diego State for his final season of college football that he was converted into a receiver. Though Curtis said he asked the coaches at Cal to make him a receiver during his time there, it was Don Coryell who allowed Curtis to transition to his natural position as a receiver.

3. Pat McInally was a true jack-of-all-trades for the Bengals during his 10-year NFL career. He was mostly a punter for Cincinnati during his tenure, but he was also a backup

receiver for the team and caught 57 passes for 808 yards and five touchdowns during his career. The Bengals even drafted McInally as a receiver and were told by a scout for the team that his future was at receiver and not punter. Instead, he led the NFL twice in punting average (1978 and 1981) after missing his rookie year due to an injury he suffered at the College All-Star Game.

4. Cris Collinsworth has become internet famous for his memes and jokes as an analyst on NBC's *Sunday Night Football* coverage, a continuation of his personality from his playing days. When Collinsworth attended the NFL Combine, he said the parading of the prospects through the room to be weighed and measured felt like a meat auction, so he decided to spice it up a bit by grabbing a pair of the offensive linemen's shorts to wear. The extra-large shorts didn't do his figure any favors, but it elicited laughter from the assembled coaches.

5. Eddie Brown missed the first 18 days of training camp while negotiating his contract, but he made up for lost time during his first season with the Bengals. In a draft class that included Jerry Rice, Brown was named the NFL's Rookie of the Year in 1985 after catching 53 passes for 942 yards in his first year in the league. Brown would only reach 1,000 yards once in a season with the Bengals before a neck injury forced him to retire in 1992.

6. Carl Pickens made a tremendous impact on the field for the Bengals, but he also made a big one off the field. After

Pickens made critical comments about the Bengals from 1998 to 2000, Cincinnati began adding a "loyalty clause" to rookie contracts, forbidding players to speak ill of the franchise publicly in the first few seasons of the contract. The NFLPA challenged the language in court, but the arbiter ruled that it could be in the contract if the player agreed to it. The clause caused major headaches for the Bengals in negotiations as the Brown family attempted to protect its brand.

7. Though many label Peter Warrick a draft bust because he didn't live up to his billing as the 4th overall pick, his quarterbacks played a part in that. With Akili Smith and Jon Kitna at the helm of the Bengals offense, Warrick produced two of the most inefficient seasons for a receiver in NFL history. Of the receivers with at least 125 targets since 1992, Warrick is one of only two receivers through 2019 who averaged less than five yards per target, and he did it twice in 2000 and again in 2001. In his first two years in the league, Warrick averaged just 4.79 yards per target, the worst average of anyone over a two-year span.

8. Chad Johnson was known for plenty of antics during his career in Cincinnati, but the standout receiver definitely cared. He would consistently call offensive coordinator Hue Jackson and head coach Marvin Lewis in the middle of the night. Sometimes the message was a simple, "Hey, coach, I'm open," then he would hang up. Other times he would bother Jackson for the game plan mere hours before the offense had its meeting to go over the game

plan. Quarterback Jon Kitna also told a story about Johnson being in tears in the locker room after a pass bounced off Johnson and was intercepted, sealing defeat. Johnson said he was too tired, which is why he didn't hold onto the football, and Kitna said Johnson doubled down on his conditioning after that moment to ensure it wouldn't happen again.

9. T.J. Houshmandzadeh never finished high school and wasn't all that interested in playing football until he arrived at Cerritos College. He was brought along as a bonus to friend Glenn Pope, who was recruited by the junior college as a receiver. However, Pope broke his foot that first season, and the coaches were going to cut Houshmandzadeh, but instead, the wideout took over and impressed the coaches. His performance led to Houshmandzadeh going to play at Oregon State and eventually the NFL with the Bengals.

10. A.J. Green made an instant impact in Cincinnati in a way no receiver had previously done in the NFL. Green was named to the Pro Bowl in each of his first seven seasons, the first receiver in five decades to accomplish that feat. He was nicknamed "The Martian" by teammates because he continuously made plays like he was from another planet. And he also took care of his teammates, purchasing a car for fellow receiver Andrew Hawkins each year Hawkins was in the league with Green, telling his teammate, "If A.J. Green is going to have a deal, then Hawk has to have a car, too."

CHAPTER 6:

TRENCH WARFARE

QUIZ TIME!

1. Which offensive lineman holds the Bengals' record for most Pro Bowl appearances, with 11?

   a. Anthony Muñoz
   b. Bob Johnson
   c. Willie Anderson
   d. Andrew Whitworth

2. Max Montoya is the only Bengals interior lineman to ever be named to the Pro Bowl.

   a. True
   b. False

3. Which of these offensive tackles was NOT a top-10 draft choice by the Bengals?

   a. Andre Smith
   b. Vern Holland
   c. Levi Jones
   d. Willie Anderson

4. How many touchdown passes did Anthony Muñoz catch in his career with the Bengals?

   a. 1
   b. 2
   c. 3
   d. 4

5. Bob Johnson was the Bengals' starter at center for the first 94 games of the franchise's history. Who replaced him for the final four games of the 1974 season to become Cincinnati's second starting center?

   a. Vern Holland
   b. Pat Matson
   c. Howard Fest
   d. John Shinners

6. Who got hurt in 1979, bringing Bob Johnson out of retirement to play five more games with the Bengals?

   a. Mack Mitchell
   b. Blair Bush
   c. Mark Donahue
   d. Dave Lapham

7. Anthony Muñoz was named to the Pro Bowl as a rookie.

   a. True
   b. False

8. How many times was Anthony Muñoz named a First Team All-Pro during his 12 years with the Bengals?

a. 7

b. 8

c. 9

d. 10

9. Which team tried to sign Rich Braham as a restricted free agent, forcing the Bengals to lock down their starting center for the next decade?

a. New York Jets

b. Baltimore Ravens

c. New England Patriots

d. Pittsburgh Steelers

10. In which season was Willie Anderson NOT named a First Team All-Pro?

a. 2005

b. 2004

c. 2003

d. 2002

11. What is the Bengals' record for most sacks by a player in a single game?

a. 7

b. 6.5

c. 5.5

d. 5

12. Who was the first Bengals defensive lineman to be named a First Team All-Pro?

a. Geno Atkins

b. Eddie Edwards

c. Mike Reid

d. Coy Bacon

13. The Bengals are the only team in the AFC that hasn't had a defender named the Associated Press Defensive Player of the Year or the AP Defensive Rookie of the Year.

a. True

b. False

14. Who holds the Bengals' record for most Pro Bowl appearances for a defender?

a. Reggie Williams

b. Geno Atkins

c. Carlos Dunlap

d. Tim Krumrie

15. In which year did Vontaze Burfict stay out of trouble long enough to be named to the Pro Bowl?

a. 2013

b. 2014

c. 2015

d. 2016

16. Eddie Edwards is the Bengals' all-time leader in sacks with how many?

a. 78.5

b. 81

c. 83.5

d. 86

17. What is Coy Bacon's franchise record for most sacks in a single season, according to the team?

    a. 19.5
    b. 20
    c. 21.5
    d. 22

18. Reggie Williams holds the Bengals' record for most consecutive games played by a non-specialist when he appeared in how many straight games for the franchise from 1980 to 1989?

    a. 149
    b. 146
    c. 142
    d. 137

19. In which year did Carlos Dunlap set his career high, with 13.5 sacks?

    a. 2015
    b. 2016
    c. 2017
    d. 2018

20. Geno Atkins was named to the Hall of Fame's all-decade team for the 2010s.

    a. True
    b. False

QUIZ ANSWERS

1. A – Anthony Muñoz

2. A – True

3. B – Vern Holland

4. D – 4

5. C – Howard Fest

6. B – Blair Bush

7. B – False

8. C – 9

9. C – New England Patriots

10. D – 2002

11. D – 5

12. C – Mike Reid

13. B – False

14. B – Geno Atkins

15. A – 2013

16. C – 83.5

17. D – 22

18. D – 137

19. A – 2015

20. A – True

DID YOU KNOW?

1. Bob Johnson was ready to retire in 1978 after playing 152 games for the Bengals as the team's center. The team even retired his number after that final home game in 1978 in honor of his contributions to the franchise. However, that turned out to not be his final game in a Bengals uniform. After Blair Bush was injured in 1979, the Bengals persuaded Johnson to come out of retirement to be the team's long snapper on punts, field goals, and extra points. Johnson said he felt like he owed the organization the courtesy of playing those five games, but he wasn't in the physical shape to sustain the hits of a typical center after dropping 35 pounds in retirement.

2. Dave Lapham was accepted by all eight Ivy League schools but, instead, attended Syracuse to play football. Lapham said his mother was disappointed that he didn't take the chance to study at a prestigious institution, but he wanted the best combination of football and academics, which led him to Syracuse. It isn't the only tough decision Lapham has made in his career. The veteran lineman also decided against following Forrest Gregg to Green Bay as an offensive line coach after retiring in 1983, while also turning down several other offers from college programs.

3. Anthony Muñoz began his Bengals career as the second-string tackle despite being a 1ˢᵗ round pick. Of course, that

role as a backup lasted just three days before he took over as the starter, where he stayed for every game in his career. In his first preseason game, Muñoz was so dominant that he blocked Broncos defensive end Brison Manor off the field on one play. That dominance came even though Bengals line coach Jim McNally had Muñoz playing in a right-handed stance that first season, which was unnatural for Muñoz, who then became even better when he switched hands after that rookie year.

4. Rich Braham's tenure in Cincinnati was almost far shorter than the 13 years he ended up playing for the Bengals. Cincinnati claimed Braham off waivers midway through the 1994 season, but he played just three games at guard before he injured his ankle in the 1995 preseason and missed the entire year. After playing well in 1996, the Patriots offered the restricted free agent a lucrative contract that Cincinnati matched, altering the face of their offensive line for the next decade. Braham started at guard in 1997 and 1998 before making the switch to center, where he played for the final seven years of his career.

5. Willie Anderson was a cornerstone of the Bengals' offensive line for 12 years. He had just 13 holding penalties called against him in his career, and he allowed just one sack in 15 career games against pass rushers currently in the Hall of Fame. Buffalo's Bruce Smith is the only one to have slipped past Anderson, doing so in the tackle's rookie season in a game the Bills were winning by two scores late in the fourth quarter. However, Anderson

was at his best as a run blocker, helping pave the way for Corey Dillon and Rudi Johnson to combine for nine 1,000-yard seasons in a 10-year span.

6. Reggie Williams was instrumental after his career was over in developing the ESPN Wide World of Sports Complex at Walt Disney World Resort in Florida. He was hired to develop a business strategy for Disney World to compete in the sports market, and he pushed through the concept for the athletics complex despite skepticism throughout the company. As Disney's vice president for sports attractions—the first black person to hold the title of vice president at Disney World—Williams was instrumental in closing the deals to bring Atlanta Braves spring training, Tampa Bay Buccaneers training camp, and several other major sporting events to the complex before he retired in 2007.

7. Tim Krumrie changed the course of NFL history with his stubborn, never-quit attitude on the field. After being blocked well during a 1992 game against Green Bay, Krumrie crawled through the line of scrimmage to try to get pressure on the quarterback. Don Majkowski was stepping to throw the ball when Krumrie grabbed a hold of his ankle and tried to drag down the quarterback. Majkowski went to the ground, and his ankle snapped as he tore the tendons in his ankle, meaning the Packers had to turn to their backup quarterback to finish the game. And that is how Brett Favre started his streak of consecutive games played for the Packers.

8. Eddie Edwards is the Bengals' sack king with 83.5 sacks, though the NFL only credits him with 47.5, the amount he had after the stat became official. However, the Bengals calculated he had 36 from his entrance in the league in 1977 through 1981, the last year before sacks were officially introduced as a stat. Carlos Dunlap was supposed to break his record, and Edwards had resigned himself to the fact his record was going to be broken, but Dunlap forced his way out of Cincinnati just one sack shy of Edwards's record.

9. Few players have brought as much controversy with them on the field over the past decade as Vontaze Burfict. His anger issues caused many college programs to pass on him, and he was undrafted because of those issues and a failed drug test despite having 1st round talent. During his career in Cincinnati, Burfict was suspended three times for a total of 10 games and was fined on nine other occasions. When he was on the field, that tenacity and aggressive play was appreciated by fans, but, when Burfict crossed the line, the whole sports world was sucked into the drama that Burfict brought onto himself.

10. As Geno Atkins became more popular in Cincinnati for his play on the field, he remained mostly anonymous off the field. Despite being a 6-foot-1, 300-pound lineman, Atkins would make a game out of making people guess which position he played when they identified him as an NFL player. Most of the responses tended to be linebacker, which makes sense, considering he is an interior defensive

lineman who rushes the quarterback like a linebacker. Atkins's 75.5 sacks in 11 seasons with the Bengals puts him third on the franchise's career list, just eight behind Eddie Edwards.

CHAPTER 7:

NO AIR ZONE

QUIZ TIME!

1. The seven players had 20 or more interceptions during their careers in Cincinnati.

   a. True
   b. False

2. Who was the last player to tie the Bengals' record with three interceptions in a game?

   a. Tory James
   b. Deltha O'Neal
   c. Johnathan Joseph
   d. Leon Hall

3. Which of these Bengals defensive backs did not have a 100-plus-yard interception return in his career?

   a. Louis Breeden
   b. Dre Kirkpatrick
   c. David Fulcher
   d. Artrell Hawkins

4. Who holds the Bengals' record for most interceptions in a single season, with 10?

   a. Reggie Nelson
   b. Ken Riley
   c. Deltha O'Neal
   d. Leon Hall

5. Who was the Bengal who most recently led the NFL in interceptions?

   a. Dre Kirkpatrick
   b. Reggie Nelson
   c. Ken Riley
   d. Leon Hall

6. In which year did the Bengals set their franchise record with 34 interceptions in a season?

   a. 1981
   b. 1988
   c. 1996
   d. 2005

7. What is the Bengals' team record for most interceptions in a single game, set in 1971 against the Chargers and tied five years later against the Jets?

   a. 5
   b. 6
   c. 7
   d. 8

8. Which of these quarterbacks has NOT thrown five interceptions in a game against Cincinnati during his career?

a. Brett Favre

b. Daunte Culpepper

c. Kyle Orton

d. Joe Namath

9. The Bengals have held a team to negative net passing yards.

a. True

b. False

10. What is the Bengals' record for most pick-sixes in a career?

a. 5

b. 6

c. 7

d. 8

11. Ken Riley has exactly twice as many career interceptions as any other Bengals player.

a. True

b. False

12. Ken Riley holds the Bengals' record for most games played for the franchise. How many games did Riley play for Cincinnati?

a. 199

b. 204

c. 207

d. 211

13. How many punt return touchdowns did Lemar Parrish score during his career in Cincinnati?

    a. 3
    b. 4
    c. 5
    d. 6

14. Who was the first Bengals defensive back to be named a First Team All-Pro?

    a. Tommy Casanova
    b. Ken Riley
    c. Louis Breeden
    d. Lemar Parrish

15. From which school did the Bengals draft David Fulcher in 1986?

    a. Washington
    b. Oregon State
    c. Arizona
    d. Arizona State

16. In which year did Tory James set his career high by intercepting eight passes in a season for the Bengals?

    a. 2007
    b. 2006
    c. 2005
    d. 2004

17. How did the Bengals acquire Deltha O'Neal before the 2004 season?

a. Trade

b. Veteran free agent

c. NFL Draft

d. Undrafted free agent

18. Johnathan Joseph was voted into the Pro Bowl during his career in Cincinnati.

    a. True

    b. False

19. Who was the last Bengals defensive back with five interceptions in a season?

    a. Darius Phillips

    b. Reggie Nelson

    c. Dre Kirkpatrick

    d. Shawn Williams

20. How many cornerbacks did the Bengals draft in the 1st round between 2006 and 2016?

    a. 3

    b. 4

    c. 5

    d. 6

QUIZ ANSWERS

1. A – True

2. D – Leon Hall

3. C – David Fulcher

4. C – Deltha O'Neal

5. B – Reggie Nelson

6. C – 1996

7. B – 6

8. D – Joe Namath

9. A – True

10. A – 5

11. B – False

12. C – 207

13. B – 4

14. A – Tommy Casanova

15. D – Arizona State

16. D – 2004

17. A – Trade

18. B – False

19. D – Shawn Williams

20. C – 5

DID YOU KNOW?

1. There is really no doubt as to who the best defensive back in Bengals history is. Ken Riley laps the field when it comes to takeaways, with 65 interceptions; one shy of being exactly twice as many as Louis Breeden, who is in second place. Those 65 picks are the most for any player for a single team since the Bengals came into existence, and Riley returned five of those for touchdowns. He had at least five interceptions in each of seven seasons, including eight in his final season as a professional when he was named a First Team All-Pro for the only time in his career.

2. For four decades, Lemar Parrish held the Bengals' record for most Pro Bowl appearances by a defensive player with six selections during his eight years in Cincinnati. He currently ranks fifth in franchise history with 25 interceptions, and he returned four of those picks for touchdowns. Bengals owner Mike Brown called Parrish "the most talented cornerback we ever had" due to his athleticism and speed that allowed him to stick with receivers. However, like many other Bengals stars, Parrish asked out of Cincinnati when he felt like the team was underpaying him for his accomplishments on the field.

3. In addition to his exploits on defense, Lemar Parrish was a game-changer on special teams. He holds the Bengals'

record with four punt return touchdowns, and he also returned a kickoff for a touchdown in 1970. The same day he returned that kickoff 95 yards for a touchdown, he also returned a blocked kick 83 yards for a score as the Bengals scored 31 points on special teams in a win over Buffalo. His six special team touchdowns account for nearly half of the 13 total touchdowns he scored for the Bengals during his career.

4. Louis Breeden held the record for the longest play in Bengals history for 39 years, and it was all a happy accident. In what turned out to be an AFC Championship game preview in 1981 against the Chargers, Breeden was in the right place at the right time as a San Diego receiver fell down. Breeden intercepted the pass and raced 102 yards behind his defensive line, who paved the way with excellent blocking, for a touchdown. It was one of three takeaways he had that day against the Chargers with two interceptions and a fumble recovery.

5. David Fulcher wanted to play wide receiver in college, but all of the college programs that recruited him told the star high school receiver that they wanted him at safety. Arizona State defensive backs coach Willie Shaw told Fulcher he could play wideout at ASU, but that experiment lasted just three days before he was converted to a safety. Fulcher had another issue when it came to his transition to the NFL with some teams viewing him as an outside linebacker because of his size. The Bengals, though, viewed him as a safety, and defensive coordinator Dick LeBeau

warned people, "Get ready for the biggest strong safety ever in football." It was the right call, too, as Fulcher ranks third in team history with 31 interceptions.

6. The 2005 Bengals secondary was one of the most opportunistic groups in team history. Deltha O'Neal set the team record with 10 interceptions, also tying for the league lead in the category, accounting for nearly a third of Cincinnati's 31 interceptions that season, the second most in team history. O'Neal tied the team record for interceptions in a game in the second game of the season with three against Minnesota, setting the tone for the rest of the season. Playing opposite O'Neal was Tory James, who had five picks in 2005, and middle linebacker Odell Thurman also added five interceptions.

7. Leon Hall wasn't even good enough to make the freshman football team at his high school, being placed on the B team that played an extra quarter once the freshman football game was completed. Not only did he end up becoming a two-year starter in high school, he did so with a tough environment at home, living with his three sisters and eight nieces and nephews, ranging in age from 12 to 18, after his mother died of a heart attack. Despite the challenge, Hall had a load of success with the Bengals over nine seasons with the franchise. He is fourth in team history with 26 interceptions after being a 1st round pick in the 2007 Draft.

8. Reggie Nelson had a special season in 2015 when he was named to his first Pro Bowl after tying for the NFL lead

with eight interceptions. Many of those picks came toward the end of the season when the safety tied Ken Riley's record with an interception in five straight games. Two games before the streak began, Nelson intercepted Ben Roethlisberger twice, giving him seven interceptions in a seven-game span that season.

9. In 2017, Dre Kirkpatrick was cruising to his third career pick-six after stepping in front of a Brock Osweiler pass and sprinting out of the end zone and up the sideline. Yet, unprovoked, Kirkpatrick coughed up the football at the Denver 15-yard line and recovered his own fumble at the one. That 101-yard return was the longest non-scoring interception return in NFL history at the time and became the butt of many jokes in the victorious postgame locker room. After recovering the fumble, Kirkpatrick was actually ill on the sidelines, a combination of his fatigue and the Denver altitude, and though he didn't miss any game time, he was gifted another oxygen tank on the team charter home from Denver.

10. Marvin Lewis was a defensive coordinator before becoming the Bengals' head coach, and his time in Cincinnati reflected that background. In the 35 seasons preceding Lewis's arrival, the Bengals had just three cornerbacks reach the Pro Bowl. Yet, in Lewis's tenure with the Bengals, Cincinnati had three Pro Bowl cornerbacks and drafted another, Johnathan Joseph. Reggie Nelson also went to the Pro Bowl as a safety for Lewis's Bengals teams,

meaning four of the 10 Bengals defensive backs who have made the Pro Bowl did so while playing for Lewis.

CHAPTER 8:

SUPER BOWL SHUFFLE

QUIZ TIME!

1. Which city hosted the Super Bowl the first time the Bengals played in the game?

   a. San Diego

   b. New Orleans

   c. Miami

   d. Detroit

2. The Bengals have never scored in the first half of a Super Bowl.

   a. True

   b. False

3. What was the total margin of defeat in the Bengals' two Super Bowl losses?

   a. 14 points

   b. 11 points

   c. 9 points

   d. 6 points

4. How many regular-season victories did the Bengals have in both 1981 and 1988?

    a. 12
    b. 14
    c. 13
    d. 11

5. What was the score of San Francisco's win in the regular-season meeting between the 49ers and Bengals in 1981 in what turned out to be a Super Bowl preview?

    a. 17-0
    b. 27-14
    c. 20-17
    d. 21-3

6. Who recovered the fumble on the opening kickoff to give Cincinnati excellent starting field position in Super Bowl XVI?

    a. John Simmons
    b. Jim LeClair
    c. Steve Kreider
    d. Bryan Hicks

7. How many passing yards did Joe Montana accumulate in Super Bowl XVI when he was named Super Bowl MVP?

    a. 146
    b. 152
    c. 157
    d. 163

8. Who was the leading rusher in Super Bowl XVI?

    a. Pete Johnson
    b. Earl Cooper
    c. Ken Anderson
    d. Ricky Patton

9. The Bengals had more turnovers than punts in their Super Bowl XVI loss.

    a. True
    b. False

10. Who busted through the line to record Cincinnati's only sack in its Super Bowl XVI loss?

    a. Eddie Edwards
    b. Glenn Cameron
    c. Reggie Williams
    d. Ross Browner

11. Joe Montana's winning touchdown pass to John Taylor came with how much time left on the clock?

    a. 43 seconds
    b. 39 seconds
    c. 34 seconds
    d. 28 seconds

12. The Bengals never trailed in Super Bowl XXIII until that Joe Montana touchdown pass late in the fourth quarter.

    a. True
    b. False

13. Which Bengals receiver set the record for most receptions in a Super Bowl in Super Bowl XVI only for Jerry Rice to tie the mark in Super Bowl XXIII against Cincinnati?

   a. Isaac Curtis
   b. Cris Collinsworth
   c. Dan Ross
   d. Charles Alexander

14. How many times did the 49ers sack Boomer Esiason in Super Bowl XXIII?

   a. 5
   b. 4
   c. 3
   d. 6

15. Which of these players did NOT start in both Super Bowls for the Bengals?

   a. Reggie Williams
   b. Cris Collinsworth
   c. Anthony Muñoz
   d. Max Montoya

16. Which of these Bengals never scored in a Super Bowl?

   a. Pete Johnson
   b. Ken Anderson
   c. Stanford Jennings
   d. Dan Ross

17. Who has scored the most points in the Super Bowl in Bengals history?

a. Chris Bahr

b. Doug Pelfrey

c. Jim Breech

d. Dan Ross

18. What is the nickname given to the 1982 AFC Championship game the Bengals won to advance to their first Super Bowl?

a. Breezer Bowl

b. Freezer Bowl

c. Riverfront Rumble

d. Tundra Tussle

19. What team did Cincinnati beat in the AFC Championship game to advance to Super Bowl XXIII in 1989?

a. Denver Broncos

b. Seattle Seahawks

c. Los Angeles Raiders

d. Buffalo Bills

20. The Bengals have not won a playoff game since winning the AFC Championship game to advance to Super Bowl XXIII.

a. True

b. False

QUIZ ANSWERS

1. D – Detroit

2. B – False

3. C – 9 points

4. A – 12

5. D – 21-3

6. A – John Simmons

7. C – 157

8. D – Ricky Patton

9. A – True

10. D – Ross Browner

11. C – 34 seconds

12. B – False

13. C – Dan Ross

14. A – 5

15. B – Cris Collinsworth

16. A – Pete Johnson

17. C – Jim Breech

18. B – Freezer Bowl

19. D – Buffalo Bills

20. B – False

DID YOU KNOW?

1. One of the pivotal moments of Super Bowl XVI came late in the third quarter when the Bengals had three cracks at the end zone from the San Francisco one-yard line while trailing 20-7. On second down, receiver David Verser went in motion and was supposed to block the outside linebacker on the play but ran right past his mark, allowing the 49ers to stuff Pete Johnson for no gain. The following down, Charles Alexander cut his route short and was met at the goal line by a horde of defenders and didn't score. On fourth down, the Bengals tried to run over the right side of the line, but the 49ers were ready for the run between the tackles and stuffed it to complete a critical goal-line stand.

2. One of the biggest regrets about that goal-line stand was that the Bengals did not attempt one of their naked bootlegs with Ken Anderson. Guard Dave Lapham said Anderson would have had an easy walk into the end zone on fourth down had Cincinnati called the play, given how San Francisco lined up to stop Pete Johnson. Anderson, though, said hindsight is 20/20, and he trusted Pete Johnson to be able to bust through for that final yard, so he doesn't regret the decision. Anderson also mentioned that he had talked about running the bootleg later with 49ers defensive coordinator Chuck Studley, who told

Anderson that San Francisco was waiting on the fake as well and had that possibility built into the play call.

3. Turnovers tend to hurt teams in big moments, and the Bengals had two crucial turnovers inside the red zone that cost them 14 points. The 49ers fumbled the opening kickoff, giving Cincinnati prime field position to score first in Super Bowl XVI. Instead, Ken Anderson was sacked and then threw an interception in the end zone after starting with a first-and-goal on the five-yard line. That led to San Francisco marching down the field for the opening touchdown, and its second touchdown was also the result of a Bengals miscue. That time, Anderson hit Cris Collinsworth for a 19-yard gain inside the 10-yard line, but Collinsworth fumbled, and San Francisco marched 92 yards to take a 14-0 lead.

4. The Bengals couldn't have played much worse in the first half of Super Bowl XVI. Cincinnati was outgained 209-99 in the first half, and the 20-0 lead San Francisco built at halftime was the largest deficit in the first 21 Super Bowls. The tide changed in the second half, as the Bengals blitzed the 49ers and kept San Francisco's offense off-balanced in limiting the 49ers to 66 yards in the second half while Cincinnati's offense racked up 257 yards.

5. Super Bowl XVI was the first Super Bowl in history to be played in a traditionally cold winter climate. The Detroit area even welcomed the game with some snow and a wind chill factor that dipped to 21 below zero on game

day. It still holds the record for the coldest temperature at a domed Super Bowl, with the official report being 13 degrees Fahrenheit at kickoff. Super Bowl XVI was also the first time a national television broadcast used a telestrator to help the color analyst explain replays, and there was no one better than John Madden to be the pioneer of the new technology.

6. Bengals fans likely won't forget the images of Tim Krumrie's gruesome injury that knocked him out of Super Bowl XXIII just seven plays into the contest. Krumrie broke through a double-team block to try and stuff Roger Craig at the line of scrimmage, but his leg twisted the wrong direction, resulting in a compound, segmented fracture that included four breaks. Not wanting to miss out on the game or the experience, Krumrie refused to go to the hospital and barely took any painkillers in order to remember the moment, even if he was stuck in the locker room at Joe Robbie Stadium.

7. Not only was the opposition the same for the Bengals in their second Super Bowl appearance but so too were the record performances. In Super Bowl XVI, Dan Ross set a record with 11 receptions in the loss. In Super Bowl XXIII, Jerry Rice tied Ross's record by catching 11 passes and became the only receiver in Super Bowl history to eclipse 200 yards receiving. It would take another 16 years for someone to catch 11 passes in a Super Bowl again, and their record was broken 25 years after Rice tied it.

8. One of the highlights of the Bengals' run to Super Bowl XXIII was the invention of the "Ickey Shuffle" by Bengals running back Ickey Woods. It started after Woods did an end-zone dance in a game against the Browns that teammate Rickey Dixon said was terrible. So Woods retooled his dance and showcased it to the world in October 1988 in a game against the Jets. Soon, the dance spread throughout the country as Woods scored 15 touchdowns during the 1988 season to help lead Cincinnati to the Super Bowl as a rookie.

9. The Bengals faced plenty of distractions not far away from where the team was staying in Miami for Super Bowl XXIII. After arriving in South Florida for the game, there was an incident within a few hundred yards of the Bengals' hotel in which a Hispanic police officer shot and killed a black motorcyclist. This caused a protest in which rocks and bottles were thrown consistently at police officers trying to calm the situation, dominating the headlines and attention in a week when Cincinnati was trying to focus on winning a football game. Boomer Esiason said the police told the team to make sure they knew where they were going if they left the hotel and to be wary of making a wrong turn and entering into harm's way.

10. Adding to the distractions ahead of Super Bowl XXIII was the plight of Stanley Wilson, who had battled drug addiction for much of his NFL career. Wilson missed the final team meeting on the night before the game, and his

roommate, Eddie Brown, told the coaches that he was in the room and wouldn't come out. The staff and trainers found Wilson in the bathtub naked and high on cocaine and were able to coax Wilson into clothes and called for an ambulance. However, Wilson ran away from the hotel and was not seen for a few days, leaving coach Sam Wyche to address the situation with the team, and his absence was felt in another tough defeat to the 49ers.

CHAPTER 9:

SHINING THE BUSTS

QUIZ TIME!

1. The Bengals have had more Hall-of-Famers play for them than the Baltimore Ravens have.

   a. True
   b. False

2. Who was the first player with ties to the Bengals to be enshrined in the Hall of Fame?

   a. Terrell Owens
   b. Ken Anderson
   c. Anthony Muñoz
   d. Charlie Joiner

3. How many Hall-of-Famers have coached for the Bengals in the franchise's history?

   a. 3
   b. 4
   c. 5
   d. 6

4. Which of these famous Bengals items is NOT stored at the Hall of Fame?

    a. Seat from Riverfront Stadium
    b. Shovel from Paul Brown Stadium groundbreaking
    c. Boomer Esiason's jersey from Super Bowl XXXIII
    d. Football from first kickoff to Bengals game

5. The Pro Football Hall of Fame also displays a watercolor painting of which famous Bengals player?

    a. Boomer Esiason
    b. Archie Griffin
    c. Isaac Curtis
    d. Ken Anderson

6. Anthony Muñoz is the only Hall-of-Famer ever drafted by the Bengals.

    a. True
    b. False

7. Which position did Anthony Muñoz play on the Southern California baseball team that won the College World Series in 1978?

    a. Catcher
    b. First base
    c. Pitcher
    d. Center field

8. How many games did Anthony Muñoz miss due to injury during his professional career?

a. 0

b. 3

c. 7

d. 11

9. How many times did Anthony Muñoz appear on the Hall of Fame ballot before finally being inducted into Canton?

   a. 4

   b. 3

   c. 2

   d. 1

10. In which year was Anthony Muñoz inducted into the Hall of Fame?

    a. 1999

    b. 1998

    c. 1997

    d. 1996

11. What was Paul Brown's last year coaching the Cleveland Browns before being fired, giving him the reason to found a professional football team in Cincinnati?

    a. 1965

    b. 1964

    c. 1963

    d. 1962

12. Paul Brown was inducted into the Hall of Fame after the Bengals played their first game.

    a. True

    b. False

13. Which college team did Paul Brown coach before being lured to the NFL by the Cleveland Browns?

    a. Penn State
    b. Notre Dame
    c. Ohio State
    d. Michigan

14. What was the most catches Charlie Joiner had in his three and a half seasons with the Bengals?

    a. 37
    b. 42
    c. 46
    d. 49

15. What position was Charlie Joiner drafted to play when he entered the league out of Grambling?

    a. Running back
    b. Quarterback
    c. Tight end
    d. Defensive back

16. In which city did Terrell Owens make his Hall of Fame acceptance speech after spurning the official ceremony in Canton?

    a. Cleveland, Ohio
    b. San Francisco, California
    c. Chattanooga, Tennessee
    d. Alexander City, Alabama

17. Terrell Owens led the Bengals in receiving during his only season with the team.

    a. True
    b. False

18. Who is the only other Bengals player, not named Anthony Muñoz, to be named a finalist for induction?

    a. Corey Dillon
    b. Willie Anderson
    c. Ken Riley
    d. Ken Anderson

19. Who was the former Bengal most recently named a semifinalist for the Hall of Fame?

    a. Terrell Owens
    b. Willie Anderson
    c. Corey Dillon
    d. Chad Johnson

20. In which year did the Bengals introduce a Ring of Honor to celebrate the best players in franchise history?

    a. 2021
    b. 2011
    c. 2001
    d. 1991

QUIZ ANSWERS

1. B – False

2. D – Charlie Joiner

3. A – 3

4. C – Boomer Esiason's jersey from Super Bowl XXXIII

5. C – Isaac Curtis

6. A – True

7. C – Pitcher

8. B – 3

9. D – 1

10. B – 1998

11. D – 1962

12. B – False

13. C – Ohio State

14. A – 37

15. D – Defensive Back

16. C – Chattanooga, Tennessee

17. A – True

18. D – Ken Anderson

19. B – Willie Anderson

20. A – 2021

DID YOU KNOW?

1. Paul Brown had already been inducted into the Pro Football Hall of Fame when he helped spearhead the movement to bring professional football to Cincinnati. Many of the NFL owners were upset by Art Modell's decision to fire Brown as the Browns' coach in January 1963 and tried to find a way for him to return to the league. Brown browsed and talked with various people about future AFL or NFL franchises in several different locations, but homed in on Cincinnati in 1965 as the place. Unfortunately, Brown was not awarded the 16th NFL expansion franchise because New Orleans beat out Cincinnati for the position, but soon afterward, the Bengals joined the AFL, and Brown was part of the franchise as coach for eight years and as the owner and de facto general manager until his death in 1991.

2. Anthony Muñoz was too big to play Pop Warner football in his hometown of Ontario, California, so he became a dominant pitcher and power hitter in Little League. That love of baseball translated into high school, where he was a three-sport athlete in baseball, basketball, and football. On the gridiron, Muñoz played both lines and was also the team's punter, showcasing his natural athleticism. He chose to play football at Southern California because the coaches would allow him to miss spring practice to play

baseball for the Trojans. However, injuries prevented Muñoz from taking the field for USC's baseball program in three of his four years at the school.

3. The first time Anthony Muñoz met his Bengals coach, fellow Hall-of-Famer Forrest Gregg, he put the former offensive lineman on the ground. Gregg had come to Southern California to run Muñoz through a pre-draft workout, and, toward the end of the session, Gregg was acting as the defensive lineman and rushing Muñoz. He just wanted to see how Muñoz would react to different situations, and, when Gregg faked inside and then moved outside, Muñoz naturally punched out and hit Gregg in the chest, sending him backward. Muñoz was apologetic after Gregg's head was the first thing to hit the ground, but Gregg simply smiled and told Muñoz that it was the right reaction and not to worry about it.

4. Charlie Joiner might be better known in Cincinnati as the player traded to San Diego for Coy Bacon, but Joiner was a productive receiver during his brief time with the Bengals. The Hall-of-Famer caught 82 passes for 1,463 yards in 39 games for Cincinnati and hauled in six touchdowns during that span as well. His best season for the Bengals was also his last in Cincinnati, as he gained 726 yards and scored five touchdowns on 37 catches in 1975.

5. Terrell Owens ended his Hall of Fame career by playing the 2010 season in Cincinnati, teaming up with Chad

Johnson to create what might have been the most entertaining receiver duo in NFL history. Owens led the Bengals that year with 72 catches and 983 yards in 13 games before an injury sidelined him for the final three games of the season. Owens and Johnson also hosted a television show that was broadcast on Versus (now NBC Sports Network) in which they discussed pop culture and other random topics.

6. In addition to Charlie Joiner and Terrell Owens, who played for the Bengals, three other Hall-of-Famers coached the Bengals at some point in their careers. Of that trio, only Bill Walsh, who was an assistant under Paul Brown for eight seasons from 1968 to 1975, was inducted into Canton as a coach. The other two former Bengals coaches were Forrest Gregg, who was Cincinnati's head coach from 1980 to 1983 after being inducted as a player in 1977, and Dick LeBeau, who was inducted as a player in 2010, but spent 15 years as an assistant for the Bengals before being promoted in the middle of the 2000 season to head coach, a position he held for two more seasons.

7. Though very few Bengals have busts in the Pro Football Hall of Fame, several important mementos from Bengals history are in Canton. In addition to housing all of the draft cards from the NFL Draft, the Hall of Fame possesses a metal bucket signed by Bengals owner Mike Brown and other Cincinnati community leaders from the groundbreaking of Paul Brown Stadium as well as some backrests from the seats at the former Riverfront Stadium.

Also in the collection is a full uniform from Anthony Muñoz's final year with the Bengals, one of Paul Brown's signature hats, the football used for the opening kickoff of the first Bengals regular-season game, and a Boomer Esiason jersey from this MVP season in 1988.

8. Only six players in NFL history have recorded at least 65 interceptions in their careers. Five of them are in the Hall of Fame, and the sixth is Ken Riley, who passed away in 2020. Many pundits believe that a Bengals victory in Super Bowl XVI would have propelled Riley as well as quarterback Ken Anderson into the Hall of Fame, but the two are consistently overlooked by voters. Both men require the Senior Committee from their era to advance their nomination to the full Hall of Fame voting panel in order to be elected into Canton. Anderson was twice named a finalist during his time as a modern-era nominee, joining Anthony Muñoz as the only Bengals players to be named a finalist for the Hall of Fame.

9. If neither of Cincinnati's two leading senior candidates is elected into the Hall of Fame, the only modern-era candidate with a realistic chance at the moment is Willie Anderson. The offensive tackle was named a semifinalist for the first time in 2021 in his eighth year of eligibility, one of three offensive linemen named to the 25-player list. The other two offensive linemen—Tony Boselli and Alan Faneca—were both named among the 15 finalists, and Faneca earned enough votes to be part of the class of 2021. However, many voters are excited about Anderson's

nomination and said he is a deserving candidate who should be a finalist in the years to come as he stays on the ballot a little longer.

10. The Bengals didn't have a Ring of Honor or any other team Hall of Fame until 2021, when the team released a provisional list of 17 nominees to join the inaugural class. The only two guaranteed spots in that inaugural class are Anthony Muñoz, the only Hall-of-Famer who went in as a member of the Bengals, and Paul Brown, the team's co-founder and first coach and general manager. The final class will be decided by a vote of season ticket holders and inducted sometime during the 2021 season.

CHAPTER 10:

DRAFT DAY

QUIZ TIME!

1. How many players did the Bengals select in the 1968 Expansion Draft?

    a. 20

    b. 30

    c. 40

    d. 50

2. Who was NOT part of the Bengals' original 1968 draft class, the franchise's first official draft?

    a. Ken Riley

    b. Dave Middendorf

    c. Paul Robinson

    d. Bob Trumpy

3. The first year in which the Bengals did NOT draft in the top 10 was 1970, when they drafted Mike Reid.

    a. True

    b. False

4. In which year did the Bengals use their 1st round selection to draft Isaac Curtis?

   a. 1971
   b. 1972
   c. 1973
   d. 1974

5. The Bengals had two 1st round picks in the 1976 Draft; they used the second on two-time Heisman Trophy winner Archie Griffin, but who did Cincinnati select with its first pick of the draft?

   a. Reggie Williams
   b. Glenn Cameron
   c. Bill Kollar
   d. Billy Brooks

6. In which round of the 1977 NFL Draft did the Bengals select Louis Breeden out of North Carolina Central?

   a. 10th
   b. 9th
   c. 8th
   d. 7th

7. The Bengals had multiple 1st round picks in four straight drafts from 1976 to 1979.

   a. True
   b. False

8. Which wide receiver did the Bengals draft in the 1st round in 1981 before also selecting Cris Collinsworth with their second pick in the draft?

a. Steve Kreider

b. Rodney Holman

c. David Verser

d. Mark Nichols

9. In which round of the 1983 Draft did the Bengals take a chance on Tim Krumrie out of Wisconsin?

    a. 9th

    b. 10th

    c. 11th

    d. 12th

10. Who was NOT one of the three players the Bengals drafted in the 1st round in 1984 before finally picking Boomer Esiason in the 2nd round?

    a. Brian Blados

    b. Ricky Hunley

    c. Stanford Jennings

    d. Pete Koch

11. What was the only year in which the Bengals did NOT make a selection in the 1st round of the NFL Draft?

    a. 1989

    b. 1988

    c. 1987

    d. 1986

12. In which round of the 1993 Draft did the Bengals draft Doug Pelfrey, the team's kicker for the next seven seasons?

a. 4th

b. 6th

c. 7th

d. 8th

13. The same year the Bengals drafted Dan Wilkinson with the 1st overall pick, Cincinnati also drafted Kimo von Oelhoffen.

a. True

b. False

14. In which round of the 1997 NFL Draft did the Bengals draft Corey Dillon out of Washington?

a. 6th

b. 4th

c. 3rd

15. 2nd

16. In which year did the Bengals draft Chad Johnson, Rudi Johnson, and T.J. Houshmandzadeh?

a. 2000

b. 2001

c. 2002

d. 2003

17. Who was NOT part of Cincinnati's 2006 draft class, in which the first four picks Cincinnati made played at least 150 games in the NFL?

a. Frostee Rucker

b. Robert Geathers

c. Johnathan Joseph

d. Domata Peko

18. In which year did the Bengals use a 4th round draft pick to select Geno Atkins?

    a. 2012

    b. 2011

    c. 2010

    d. 2009

19. Who did the Bengals draft with the 5th round choice they received in the Chad Johnson trade?

    a. Cobi Hamilton

    b. Rex Burkhead

    c. George Iloka

    d. Marvin Jones

20. Gio Bernard was the player Cincinnati drafted with the 1st round pick it received in the Carson Palmer trade.

    a. True

    b. False

21. In which round did the Bengals draft Joe Mixon in 2017?

    a. 2nd

    b. 3rd

    c. 4th

    d. 5th

QUIZ ANSWERS

1. C – 40

2. A – Ken Riley

3. B – False

4. C – 1973

5. D – Billy Brooks

6. D – 7th

7. A – True

8. C – David Verser

9. B – 10th

10. C – Stanford Jennings

11. A – 1989

12. D – 8th

13. A – True

14. D – 2nd

15. B – 2001

16. B – Robert Geathers

17. C – 2010

18. D – Marvin Jones

19. B – False

20. A – 2nd

DID YOU KNOW?

1. Bob Johnson was attending an engineering class when the call came that made him the first Bengals draft pick. He and his wife had waited by the phone when the draft started at 9:00 a.m., but, after about 30 minutes without the phone ringing, he left for class. When he came home, his wife had a simple question for him: "What's a Bengal?" That's how Johnson learned that he was drafted by Cincinnati, an expansion franchise about which he knew little because the Bengals never spoke with him before the draft.

2. In 1974, it was rare to see an NFL scout roaming the campus of an Ivy League school, yet a Bengals scout was dispatched to Harvard to chat with Pat McInally. The receiver and punter was an intriguing prospect for NFL teams, and Cincinnati was trying to do some research on the 6-foot-5, 210-pound pass-catcher. The first question the scout asked McInally was whether or not 11:00 p.m. was before or after midnight, and the receiver gave a complex answer that it was before midnight of the next day but after midnight on that specific day. The Bengals marked it as wrong, but the other 17 questions went well enough that Cincinnati used a 5th round pick on McInally.

3. Paul Brown played the long game when it came to drafting Ross Browner in 1978. Browner had first come

onto the Bengals owner's radar years earlier at the Ohio high school all-star game, and Brown stopped into the locker room to chat with Browner and asked him where he was going to play college football. Brown told Browner then that he would keep an eye on him. In 1978, Brown kept his word and drafted Browner with the 8th overall pick that year. He told Browner afterward, "I didn't want to play against you, so I had to pick you."

4. There were plenty of legitimate medical questions about Anthony Muñoz ahead of the 1980 NFL Draft. He had torn ligaments in his knee three times during his college career, including in his left knee in the first game of his senior year. He was denied playing in the Rose Bowl in his freshman and junior seasons because of the knee injuries, but he was determined to rehab in enough time to play in the Rose Bowl as a senior. In attendance at the 1980 Rose Bowl was Bengals owner Paul Brown and his sons—Mike, the assistant general manager, and Pete, the player personnel director. The trio witnessed a dominant effort from Muñoz that answered every question they had about Muñoz's knee, giving them the confidence to draft him with the 3rd overall pick.

5. Depending on whom you ask, the Bengals were considering drafting Cris Collinsworth in the 1st round of the 1981 Draft. As legend has it, offensive coordinator Lindy Infante literally climbed onto the table in the draft room to implore the Bengals to draft Collinsworth with the 10th overall pick. Collinsworth isn't sure that the story

is true, and Mike Brown doesn't remember it happening, either, but Brown did say Infante was passionate about Collinsworth, and there was a discussion about whether to draft Collinsworth or David Verser in the 1st round. Cincinnati decided on Verser and then was able to draft Collinsworth in the 2nd round.

6. The Bengals had three chances to pick Boomer Esiason in the 1st round, and each time they passed on the quarterback from Maryland. Esiason's slide in the 1984 NFL Draft was one of the biggest surprises of that draft year, and by the time Sam Wyche made the call to Esiason ahead of the 38th pick in the 2nd round, he could tell Esiason was upset. After asking about any off-field incident that the Bengals might not have heard about that caused the slide, Wyche asked Esiason about coming to Cincinnati. Every answer displayed anger at not being drafted sooner.

7. Within six years of appearing in the Super Bowl, the Bengals earned the 1st overall pick in the 1994 NFL Draft. They could have chosen a future Hall of Fame running back in Marshall Faulk that year but instead drafted defensive tackle Dan Wilkinson. The following year, Cincinnati made a move to return to the top overall selection in the draft and drafted highly touted running back Ki-Jana Carter with the top pick. This pick turned out worse than the Wilkinson selection, however, because a knee injury in the preseason sidetracked Carter's career, and he never fully recovered to be a productive player in

the league. Fortunately, Cincinnati's other two 1st overall picks have redeemed that narrative, with Carson Palmer's success over seven seasons and a promising first year for Joe Burrow.

8. Marvin Lewis and the Bengals weren't really scouting quarterbacks much after drafting Carson Palmer in 2003. But when Palmer threatened to retire, the team turned its focus to finding a rookie quarterback who could come in and potentially start if Palmer didn't return. Lewis and his staff had coached against Andy Dalton at the Senior Bowl in 2011, and the red-headed quarterback kept appearing in front of Lewis, whether on *Good Morning America* ahead of the Super Bowl or at the NFL Combine. Lewis told offensive coordinator Jay Gruden to start scouting Dalton, and he quickly surged to near the top of the Bengals' draft board and was their consensus top quarterback target in the 2011 Draft.

9. Joe Mixon was playing some basketball outside his home in California on a Friday in 2017 when the Bengals called to let him know they had drafted him. After soaking up the celebrations with his family, Mixon hopped on a redeye flight to Cincinnati via Atlanta, beginning an epic odyssey to his new home. The flight from San Francisco to Atlanta was delayed by more than two hours, which left Mixon minutes to get off the plane and over to the gate to board the flight to Cincinnati. He spent the next two and a half hours in Atlanta's airport waiting for the next flight to Cincinnati, and a little less than 13 hours after receiving

the call from the Bengals, he was finally on his way to his new city.

10. Joe Burrow was atop the Bengals' draft board for the 2020 NFL Draft as early as December 2019, and, over the next two months, Cincinnati did every ounce of research to make sure he was the right man for the rebuilding effort. The decision was sealed, though, in an 18-minute interview at the NFL Combine when Burrow dazzled the coaching staff with his football acumen. From there, it was a long wait for Bengals fans as the COVID-19 pandemic hit, and the NFL restructured the draft process before Cincinnati was finally able to officially draft Burrow.

CHAPTER 11:

LET'S MAKE A DEAL

QUIZ TIME!

1. How many trades did the Bengals make before playing their first game in 1968?

    a. 3

    b. 4

    c. 5

    d. 6

2. The Chicago Bears were the first non-AFL team to make a trade with Cincinnati.

    a. True

    b. False

3. To which team did the Bengals send Sam Wyche when the future coach was playing for the franchise?

    a. Kansas City Chiefs

    b. Dallas Cowboys

    c. Denver Broncos

    d. Washington Redskins

4. Who did the Bengals acquire in the 1972 trade that sent Paul Robinson and Fred Willis to Houston?

   a. Herb Adderley
   b. Mike Ditka
   c. Charlie Joiner
   d. Tom Mack

5. Which running back did the Bengals trade to New Orleans to acquire the 3rd round pick they used to draft Dave Lapham in 1974?

   a. Doug Dressler
   b. Jess Phillips
   c. Essex Johnson
   d. Joe Wilson

6. Cincinnati traded Sherman White to which team in exchange for a 1st round pick that turned into the 3rd overall pick the Bengals used to draft Eddie Edwards?

   a. Miami Dolphins
   b. New York Jets
   c. Buffalo Bills
   d. New England Patriots

7. Who was the only player Cincinnati included in the 1978 trade that sent Coy Bacon to Washington in exchange for a 1st round pick?

   a. Marvin Cobb
   b. Melvin Morgan
   c. Tommy Casanova
   d. Lemar Parrish

8. The 1st round pick the Bengals acquired in the Coy Bacon trade was used to draft Charles Alexander.

   a. True
   b. False

9. Which quarterback did Cincinnati trade to Tampa Bay in exchange for a 1st round pick that ended up being the 1st overall pick in the 1984 NFL Draft?

   a. Mike Ford
   b. Turk Schonert
   c. Jeff Christensen
   d. Jack Thompson

10. The Bengals did not hold on to the 1st overall pick in the 1984 Draft, sending it to which team in exchange for two 1st round picks, a 10th round selection, and a 1985 5th round pick?

    a. New England Patriots
    b. Houston Oilers
    c. Buffalo Bills
    d. New York Giants

11. Cincinnati traded David Verser to which team in 1985 (Though, the Bengals technically didn't receive anything in return when Verser failed to make the roster.)?

    a. Green Bay Packers
    b. New York Jets
    c. Miami Dolphins
    d. Detroit Lions

12. In which round was the draft pick the Bengals acquired along with a conditional 2nd round pick from the Jets in exchange for Boomer Esiason?

    a. 5th

    b. 4th

    c. 3rd

    d. 2nd

13. The Bengals ended up receiving the conditional 2nd round pick it acquired from the Jets in the Boomer Esiason trade.

    a. True

    b. False

14. From what team did Cincinnati acquire the top pick in the 1995 NFL Draft to select Ki-Jana Carter?

    a. St. Louis Rams

    b. Carolina Panthers

    c. Houston Oilers

    d. Jacksonville Jaguars

15. The Bengals made two trades in the 1st round of the 2004 NFL Draft. With which two teams did Cincinnati swap picks?

    a. Denver Broncos and Buffalo Bills

    b. Indianapolis Colts and Buffalo Bills

    c. Denver Broncos and St. Louis Rams

    d. St. Louis Rams and Indianapolis Colts

16. Who did the Bengals send to Jacksonville as part of the trade to acquire Reggie Nelson?

a. Nedu Ndukwe

b. Tom Nelson

c. Morgan Trent

d. David Jones

17. Both picks the Bengals received from the Raiders in the Carson Palmer trade were 2012 selections.

a. True

b. False

18. In which round was the draft pick the Bengals acquired by trading Keith Rivers to the Giants?

a. 7th

b. 6th

c. 5th

d. 4th

19. Who did the Bengals acquire from the Bills in a 2018 pre-draft trade that also included the teams swapping 1st round picks?

a. Cordy Glenn

b. Thomas Rawls

c. Preston Brown

d. Adolphus Washington

20. Which team finally was able to pry Carlos Dunlap away from Cincinnati in the middle of the 2020 NFL season?

a. San Francisco 49ers

b. Las Vegas Raiders

c. Minnesota Vikings

d. Seattle Seahawks

QUIZ ANSWERS

1. B – 4

2. A – True

3. D – Washington Redskins

4. C – Charlie Joiner

5. B – Jess Phillips

6. C – Buffalo Bills

7. D – Lemar Parrish

8. A – True

9. D – Jack Thompson

10. A – New England Patriots

11. A – Green Bay Packers

12. C – 3rd

13. B – False

14. B – Carolina Panthers

15. C – Denver Broncos and St. Louis Rams

16. D – David Jones

17. B – False

18. C – 5th

19. A – Cordy Glenn

20. D – Seattle Seahawks

DID YOU KNOW?

1. The Cincinnati Bengals traded for quarterback John Stofa in 1967 before the expansion draft or they were able to sign any other player. The Bengals gave up their first two bonus picks in the 1968 AFL Draft to Miami in exchange for the quarterback, who became the first starter in team history. In one season with the Bengals, Stofa was 2-5 as a starter and threw five touchdowns and five interceptions in 10 total appearances for the team.

2. For most of his life, Tim George never knew the Bengals traded him to the Lions for $100. The receiver was among the last cuts in the 1974 preseason, and the Bengals waived him. However, when the Browns put in a claim for George, the Bengals revoked the waiver claim and instead sent George to Detroit for the cash. It wasn't until 2020 that George found out that the Lions didn't acquire him through waivers; though, he spent just a week in Detroit before being cut and the Browns signing him.

3. Coy Bacon was part of two big blockbuster trades for the Bengals during his short stint in Cincinnati. The Bengals acquired the pass rusher in 1976 by trading future Hall-of-Famer Charlie Joiner to the Chargers for Bacon. After two years, Bacon forced his way out of Cincinnati along with cornerback Lemar Parrish in a trade with Washington for a 1st round pick that was used to select Charles Alexander.

At the time of the second trade, Bengals owner Paul Brown said Bacon was "expendable" after the team drafted Ross Browner that year.

4. One of the best trades in Bengals history came in 1984 when they shipped disgruntled running back Pete Johnson to the Chargers for James Brooks. Johnson's weight was a constant issue for the Bengals, despite his productivity, and he became more vocal in his desire to leave after Cincinnati failed to re-negotiate his contract. Instead, the Bengals traded him for the smaller, faster Brooks, who would go on to break Johnson's record for career rushing yards with the Bengals.

5. There was immense relief in Boomer Esiason's world when the Bengals finally traded him to the Jets in March 1993. The saga began the previous December when Esiason lost his starting job, and Cincinnati made it known that it wanted to trade the quarterback. However, tensions rose as the team tried to negotiate a deal with several suitors before taking the 3rd round pick from the Jets. When Esiason received the call that he had been traded to his hometown Jets, he let out a whoop and screamed, "I'm going home," releasing the frustration that had been building inside of him due to pressures on and off the field.

6. With the Bengals slated to pick 5th overall in 1995, the franchise laid out several different scenarios for itself. It had the option to trade back to 12th overall in a deal with

Philadelphia that also would have netted Cincinnati an offensive tackle. The plan if they stayed at 5th overall was to draft Kevin Carter in the 1st round and Curtis Martin in the 2nd round at 36th overall. Then they had the plans they actually carried out by trading the 5th and 36th picks to Carolina in exchange for the 1st overall selection and the right to select Ki-Jana Carter.

7. It was widely known that Corey Dillon was looking for a way out of Cincinnati in 2004, but many teams had concerns about Dillon's personality. The New England Patriots were certainly interested in the running back, but they wanted to do their due diligence, so they met with Dillon and his agent at a hotel in Connecticut to discuss how Dillon would mesh with the culture in New England. The final approval came when Bengals owner Mike Brown assured Bill Belichick, the Patriots coach and general manager, that Dillon would be a productive member of the organization and wouldn't cause trouble.

8. Shortly after the Corey Dillon trade, the Bengals made another splash by swapping 1st round picks and acquiring Deltha O'Neal in a trade with Denver. O'Neal spent three days in Cincinnati before the trade was officially announced, and many speculated he was negotiating a long-term deal with the team before the sides officially agreed to the trade. Just a year after acquiring O'Neal from the Broncos, the cornerback led the league and set a franchise record with 10 interceptions, fulfilling the potential Cincinnati saw in him after the trade.

9. Carson Palmer was ready to retire after the 2010 season if the Bengals didn't trade him, and he kept his word by not reporting to training camp in 2011. When training camp opened in July, it seemed that Palmer was simply going to retire because the Bengals showed no interest in trading the quarterback's rights anywhere unless the Bengals received at least 1st and 2nd round picks. However, Palmer never filed the paperwork, so he was officially just a holdout and training in California with former teammates T.J. Houshmandzadeh and Terrell Owens. Finally, the Raiders budged on the asking price after their starter, Jason Campbell, was injured, and they sent their 2012 1st round pick and 2013 2nd round selection to Cincinnati for Palmer.

10. It's rare when the Cincinnati Bengals and Cleveland Browns make a trade, so when it does happen, it's monumental news. It's also big news when the two teams bungle a trade, as happened in 2017 when the Browns tried to trade for quarterback A.J. McCarron. The teams agreed to the deal about 20 minutes before the 2017 trade deadline, and all that was left was notifying the NFL about the trade. Cleveland emailed its paperwork to Cincinnati, assuming the Bengals would forward it to the league for them, while the Bengals copied the Browns on their paperwork to the NFL. However, Cincinnati didn't recognize the email from the Browns executive who sent it, and, because both sides did not submit paperwork to the league, the trade never occurred.

CHAPTER 12:

WRITING THE RECORD BOOK

QUIZ TIME!

1. Who attempted a franchise record 68 passes in an overtime win over Pittsburgh?

   a. Carson Palmer

   b. Ken Anderson

   c. Jon Kitna

   d. Andy Dalton

2. Against which team did Boomer Esiason set the franchise record for passing yards in a game?

   a. Miami Dolphins

   b. Cleveland Browns

   c. Dallas Cowboys

   d. Los Angeles Rams

3. Ken Anderson still holds the Bengals' franchise record for career passing yards.

   a. True

   b. False

4. How many touchdowns did Carson Palmer throw against the Browns in 2007 to set the franchise record?

    a. 7
    b. 5
    c. 8
    d. 6

5. Against which team did Corey Dillon set the franchise record with 278 rushing yards?

    a. Tennessee Titans
    b. Denver Broncos
    c. Arizona Cardinals
    d. New York Jets

6. Who set the Bengals' record with four rushing touchdowns in a single game?

    a. Paul Robinson
    b. Pete Johnson
    c. Rudi Johnson
    d. Corey Dillon

7. Ickey Wood's 15 rushing touchdowns is a single-season record for Cincinnati.

    a. True
    b. False

8. Who holds the Bengals' record for 100-yard rushing games in a season?

    a. Corey Dillon
    b. Rudi Johnson

c. Cedric Benson

d. Pete Johnson

9. Who caught four touchdown passes in a game to take hold of the Bengals' single-game record?

a. T.J. Houshmandzadeh

b. A.J. Green

c. Marvin Jones

d. Isaac Curtis

10. How many catches did Carl Pickens have in a 1998 win over the Steelers to set the Bengals' single-game record?

a. 16

b. 15

c. 14

d. 13

11. Who holds the Bengals' career record for touchdown receptions?

a. Chad Johnson

b. Eddie Brown

c. A.J. Green

d. Carl Pickens

12. When did Carl Pickens set the franchise record with 17 touchdown catches in a season?

a. 1993

b. 1994

c. 1995

d. 1996

13. Reggie Williams is the only Bengals player with multiple safeties in his career in Cincinnati.

    a. True
    b. False

14. Though Coy Bacon is recognized by the Bengals as the holder of the franchise's single-season sack record, who has the most sacks on anyone in a season since sacks became an official stat in 1982?

    a. Ross Browner
    b. Carlos Dunlap
    c. Geno Atkins
    d. Eddie Edwards

15. Who is the only Bengals player to return two interceptions for touchdowns in the same game?

    a. Lemar Parrish
    b. Leon Hall
    c. Tommy Casanova
    d. Ken Riley

16. Since the NFL began recording the statistic in 1999, which Bengals player has the most passes defended in franchise history?

    a. Dre Kirkpatrick
    b. Leon Hall
    c. Johnathan Joseph
    d. Reggie Nelson

17. Shayne Graham holds the Bengals' record for most points in a season.

    a. True
    b. False

18. How long is Shayne Graham's franchise record for most consecutive made field goals?

    a. 17
    b. 18
    c. 20
    d. 21

19. Who was the first Bengals player to return two kickoffs for a touchdown in his career with the Bengals?

    a. Tremain Mack
    b. Stanford Jennings
    c. Eric Bieniemy
    d. Brandon Wilson

20. Kevin Huber tied Kyle Larson's franchise record in 2013 when he boomed a punt of how many yards against the Chargers?

    a. 80
    b. 77
    c. 75
    d. 74

QUIZ ANSWERS

1. C – Jon Kitna

2. D – Los Angeles Rams

3. A – True

4. D – 6

5. B – Denver Broncos

6. D – Corey Dillon

7. A – True

8. C – Cedric Benson

9. C – Marvin Jones

10. D – 13

11. A – Chad Johnson

12. C – 1995

13. B – False

14. B – Carlos Dunlap

15. A – Lemar Parrish

16. B – Leon Hall

17. B – False

18. D – 21

19. A – Tremain Mack

20. C – 75

DID YOU KNOW?

1. The oldest record in the Bengals' record book belongs to Greg Cook, who averaged 9.41 yards per attempt in 1969. It is the only record that still stands from the Bengals' original home at Nippert Stadium, and it is likely to stand for a while. The only person in the last 30 years to get near the record was Andy Dalton in 2015, but he was still almost a full yard shy of Cook's mark.

2. Boomer Esiason needed every bit of his team-record 490 passing yards on October 7, 1990. The Bengals defeated the Rams in overtime after taking a 21-0 lead early in the second quarter, and Esiason was on point with his passing. His 31 completions and 45 passing attempts are not close to the team record for those categories, and he threw just three touchdown passes in the victory but found ways to dissect the Rams' defense with his arm. The 490 yards is 43 more than Ken Anderson had in a 1975 game to set the record that Esiason broke.

3. When it comes to the Bengals' rushing records, it's safe to assume Corey Dillon's name is atop the list. In 1997, he set the Bengals' single-game rushing record with a monstrous 246-yard game against Tennessee as a rookie, scoring four times on the ground to set the Bengals' mark for rushing touchdowns in a game. That record lasted less than three years before he smashed it with a dominant performance

against Denver in 2000 to lead the Bengals to their first win of the season. He needed just 22 carries to rack up 278 rushing yards—then an NFL record as well—that October day at Paul Brown Stadium. Though the record has been eclipsed by three players, every other running back needed at least 30 carries to reach their mark ahead of Dillon.

4. In a game most Bengals fans would rather forget, their team blew a 21-point halftime lead at home and lost to the Chargers. However, November 12, 2006, was also the date of Chad Johnson's record-setting performance. Johnson caught 11 passes for 260 yards and two touchdowns, the second of which went for 74 yards to give him the Bengals' single-game record. The 260 yards he had in the game was 44 more than Eddie Brown and still stands as the Bengals' record by 33 yards over A.J. Green.

5. There is no doubt that Coy Bacon holds the Bengals' record for sacks in a season, and he set the mark in 1976. Those facts are not in dispute by Bacon, the team, or football historians. What is in question is exactly how many sacks Bacon had that year, six seasons before the NFL adopted it as an official statistic. By Bacon's count and several other sources, Bacon registered 26 sacks in that 1976 season, which would be the unofficial NFL record. The Bengals list 22 sacks that season, which would be tied for second most in a single season. Either way, it is the Bengals' record, though the NFL would say Carlos Dunlap holds the record at 13.5 sacks in 2015.

6. Antwan Odom was sort of a forgotten menace on September 9, 2009. Green Bay was so worried that day about protecting the right side of the offensive line that Odom was able to tie a Bengals record with five sacks against a rotated left side of the Packers' line. He had two sacks against Chad Clifton, a two-time Pro Bowl tackle, then had three more against Clifton's replacements after Clifton left the game with an ankle injury. Odom tied Eddie Edwards's record from 1980 against Cleveland, but former Bengals guard and current radio broadcaster Dave Lapham said he remembers Mike Reid having five sacks in a game in 1974, though it is not listed in the Bengals' record book.

7. For 13 years, Jim Breech was the man who trotted onto the field to kick for the Bengals, cementing himself atop the Bengals' scoring leaderboard. His 1,151 points is 372 more than the next closest player, buoyed by a team-record 225 made field goals. Breech also holds the record with 476 extra points made, nearly twice as many as the second-place kicker, and he holds the record with 56 extra points made in 1988.

8. Most of the Bengals' kicking records that don't belong to Jim Breech belong to Shayne Graham. Cincinnati's second-leading scorer holds the record for field goals in a game with seven, which supplies all the points in a 21-7 win over the Ravens in 2007. In that 2007 season, Graham set the team record for field goal accuracy with a 91.18% success rate after converting 21 straight kicks—also a

franchise record—but his 31 made field goals that season was eclipsed by Mike Nugent (33) in 2011. The kicker also holds the team's career accuracy record by making 86.76% of his field goal attempts.

9. The Bengals are more adept at blowing big leads than mounting comebacks from large deficits, but twice, Cincinnati rallied from 21 points down to win. The first comeback was the season opener in 1981 at Riverfront Stadium, where the Seahawks scored the first 21 points of the game to take a commanding lead after the first quarter. The Bengals, though, scored 27 points in the next three quarters while shutting out Seattle to secure the victory. In the 1995 finale at home, the Bengals trailed Minnesota 24-3 at halftime before rallying for a 27-24 victory to finish the season at 7-9.

10. The Bengals have played the Tennessee Titans franchise (which dates back to being called the Houston Oilers) 75 times. Twice those matchups fell on December 17, and, both times, the Bengals set a franchise record by scoring 61 points on the Oilers. In 1972, it was a 61-17 shellacking in which Cincinnati set the team record with 45 points in the second half. The 1989 encounter was far worse as the Bengals scored the game's first 52 points before the Oilers scored early in the fourth quarter to lose 61-7.

CONCLUSION

Congratulations on reaching the end of this odyssey through the history of the Cincinnati Bengals. We hope you reached this point feeling like you want to scream "Who Dey" from the shores of the Ohio River. Whether you learned more about your favorite NFL team or were able to expand your knowledge with behind-the-scenes information about your favorite players and moments, we hope you enjoyed this book about the Cincinnati Bengals.

We tried to highlight as many of the positives as we could about the Bengals despite the gloomy reputation the franchise has earned on and off the field. Many exceptional players have come through the locker room in Cincinnati during the team's tenure on Ohio's southern coast, and Anthony Muñoz even has a bust in Canton to prove it. The past two decades with Marvin Lewis didn't lead to any postseason success, but the Bengals were again relevant and competitive in the AFC North, which leads to hope that they can return to that position again soon. The ultimate goal, of course, is to exorcise the demons of the Super Bowl XVI and XXIII teams and actually hoist the Lombardi Trophy and bring it back to Cincinnati. And perhaps Joe Burrow will be the quarterback to lead the Bengals on that quest.

We designed this book for you, the fans, to be able to embrace your favorite team and feel closer to the players. Maybe you weren't familiar with the history of the franchise and how the Bengals came into existence, and you only caught on during this most recent run of success. Perhaps you didn't realize how well Cincinnati has drafted over the years, even if those players haven't ended up in the Hall of Fame just yet. Or just maybe we didn't stump you at all, and you proved to everyone that you are indeed the ultimate Cincinnati Bengals superfan on the planet. No matter how well you did on the quizzes, we hope we captured the spirit of the franchise and gave you even more pride in your team.

The good news for the Bengals is they almost assuredly have their next franchise quarterback in Joe Burrow. If they can continue to build a solid nucleus of skilled players around him and bulk up the offensive line to protect him, the future looks bright in Cincinnati. There are a lot of exciting young players to build around for the future. It won't take much to have the Bengals once again be competitive in the always tough AFC North, and, when that happens, Cincinnati will be primed to redeem the past failures of the franchise.

Made in the USA
Las Vegas, NV
13 March 2023

69030422R00079